ONE BUDDHA IS NOT ENOUGH

one Buddha is not enough

A STORY OF COLLECTIVE AWAKENING

Thich Nhat Hanh and the Fourfold Sangha
of Plum Village monastics and
worldwide lay practitioners

PARALLAX PRESS
BERKELEY, CALIFORNIA

Parallax Press
P.O. Box 7355
Berkeley, California 94707

Parallax Press is the publishing division of Unified Buddhist Church, Inc.

Interior photographs on pages 30, 31, 43, 47, 63, and 209 courtesy of © Michele
McCormick. "Get Well" banner photos throughout chapter four by Peter Poulides.
Jerek and Jurnee Clark on page 157 by Ann Clark. All other photographs
copyright © 2010 by the Plum Village monastics.

The material in this book comes from the summer 2009
Thich Nhat Hanh retreats at Estes Park, Colorado,
and Deer Park Monastery, California.

Cover and text design by Gopa & Ted2, Inc.

Library of Congress Cataloging-in-Publication Data

Nhât Hanh, Thích.
  One buddha is not enough : a story of collective awakening /
Thich Nhat Hanh and the Fourfold Sangha of Plum Village
monastics and worldwide lay practitioners.
    p. cm.
  ISBN 978-1-935209-63-8
  1. Enlightenment (Buddhism) 2. Spiritual life—Buddhism. I. Title.
BQ4315.N49 2010
294.3'442—dc22

                                    2010021212

2 3 4 5 6/ 14 13 12 11 10

To all awakened Buddhas and Buddhas-to-be.

In order to save our planet Earth, we must have a collective awakening. Individual awakening is not enough. That is why one Buddha is not enough.

—Thich Nhat Hanh

Contents

The Miracle of Sangha

*The Monastic Brothers and Sisters of the Plum
Village Sangha*

One Buddha Is Not Enough is a collection of essays, stories, and letters by Zen Master Thich Nhat Hanh, Buddhist monks and nuns, and laypeople. The book is dedicated to the idea that awakening is a collective process, and that we and our community are our own most important teachers.

In August of 2009, close to one thousand people gathered at the YMCA of the Rockies in Estes Park, Colorado, to enjoy a retreat with Thich Nhat Hanh, called "Thay" (teacher) by his friends, students, and the monks and nuns in his tradition. Thich Nhat Hanh lives in France and is now more than eighty years old, so the retreat was a special occasion. Eager practitioners traveled from across the United States and other parts of the world. Many made great personal and financial sacrifices to get there. Everyone had come hoping to practice mindfulness surrounded by the majesty of Rocky Mountain National Park.

When they got there, they found something completely unexpected: Thay wasn't able to attend the retreat. He had been diagnosed with a severe lung infection while he was conducting the previous retreat in Massachusetts. Thay was admitted to Massachusetts General Hospital for a two-week course of intravenous antibiotics. Seven monastic brothers and sisters stayed behind with him. The other monastics, over sixty of them, went to the YMCA of the

Rockies to prepare for the retreat as had been planned. It was to be the largest retreat that the monastics had ever conducted without Thay's physical presence.

A miracle happened at that retreat in Colorado. Each person there felt they were surrounded by many Thays, and that they themselves were also Thay. More than a thousand Thays practiced deeply and joyfully together. The retreat, titled One Buddha Is Not Enough, affectionately came to be known as One Thay Is Not Enough.

The monastic brothers and sisters held several meetings to discuss the best way to support our teacher and our retreatants. The practices of deep listening and loving speech were practiced more intensely than ever. Unified by the urgency of the situation, and by our love for Thay and our lay brothers and sisters, we experienced a profound solidarity in our brotherhood and sisterhood. Every person stepped up to take on responsibilities that we might have hesitated to in other times. We realized that the success of the retreat depended on the energy of the whole community, the whole *Sangha*, and as monastic practitioners, we had to contribute our best.

On the night of the orientation, all the monks and nuns arrived early. Without planning to, when we gathered on the stage to formally begin the retreat, we stood closely together as one unit. The entire Sangha was invited to listen to three sounds of the bell and to touch a spacious, calm place within.

From his hospital bed, Thay had written a letter for the Colorado retreatants. Brother Phap Khoi read Thay's love letter aloud very slowly and clearly: "My dear friends, I am writing to you from the Massachusetts General Hospital in Boston. I know the Sangha has manifested today in Estes Park. I miss the retreat. I miss the beautiful setting of the retreat. Especially, I miss the Sangha, I miss you...."

Tears were streaming down many faces. One retreatant later shared that in the moment she felt a strong urge to scream, but everyone around her was so still she didn't dare. Others said they felt overwhelmed with disappointment, worry, and grief. But because everyone had already agreed to stay in silence until the next day, no one could complain! The practice of Noble Silence gave everyone an opportunity to listen to the unpleasant, painful feelings inside and to embrace them. Leaving the meditation hall that first evening, everyone walked ever so quietly and attentively.

Did we come to a retreat to see Thay the way we'd go to a rock concert to see Madonna or to a basketball game to see the star center? If the rock star or sports hero doesn't show up, we're entitled to a full refund. In Colorado, some people smiled and practiced "being home in the present moment." Others were so heartbroken and angry, they didn't feel they could stay. Out of nearly a thousand participants, eight individuals went home. Those who stayed held those who needed to leave deep in the heart of their practice. We regretted that we were not able to make the retreat what they needed it to be for their own peace and healing.

Thay's absence forced us to reevaluate our intention. We could not rely on Thay for energy and inspiration. Instead, everyone came to a decision to invest ourselves wholeheartedly in the practice. Everyone walked so stably, spoke so compassionately, and thought with so much gratitude—for Thay, for each other, and for this path we were sharing. Thay was everywhere. All of us experienced Thay's presence in ourselves and in each other.

This powerful energy of our collective practice also enabled us to look into our past experiences with love, loss, expectations, and disappointments. By staying together as a Sangha, we broke through our habitual patterns of avoiding and running away from pain. Transformation and healing took place in every person, monastic and lay, beginning and long-term practitioner. We experienced directly the immense value and strength of our spiritual community, our Sangha. We realized that Thay and his teachings will continue well into the future, because we are a Sangha. Wherever we are, when we come together as a community of practice, we can generate this powerful energy of peace and healing.

Over seventy-three people signed up to help organize the retreat in Colorado next year. One teenager said that, even though Thay won't be there, he was happy there will be a retreat next year because he couldn't bear the thought of having to wait two years for the next scheduled retreat with Thay. A boy of six or seven said, "This is the best retreat of my life!" One man reported that after he left the YMCA, he shared with many friends about his wonderful experience at the retreat. At one point, he realized that he was telling them: "I was at the retreat with Thich Nhat Hanh." Indeed, we were at the retreat with Thay in the deepest possible way.

From his hospital in Boston, Thay stayed in close contact with everyone at the retreat. He wrote that it brought him great joy that the community was thriving despite his physical absence. This confirmed his belief that "in order to save the Earth, individual awakening is not enough." Thay recovered quickly and went on to lead retreats in California and New York, inspired by the stories from Colorado.

Those of us in Colorado left with a deep sense of interbeing. We know now, more than ever, that we must all see ourselves as Buddhas and Bodhisattvas, awakened beings who nurture, care for, and preserve Mother Earth for future generations. This book is a testament to the possibility and the reality of collective awakening.

Boston August 21, 2009   ①

Dear Friends and Co-practitioners
at the Retreat One Buddha is not enough
Estes Park, Co.

My dear friends,
I am writing to you from the Massachusetts General Hospital
in Boston. I know the Sangha has manifested today in
Estes Park. I miss the Retreat. I miss the beautiful setting
of the Retreat. Especially I miss the Sangha, I miss you.
I always enjoy sitting with the Sangha, walking with the
Sangha, breathing with the Sangha. The joy of being together,
sharing the Dharma and the Practice together is always
very nourishing and healing.
But i do not suffer, because i know i am taking care
of myself. And taking care of myself is to take care of
you. The doctors here decided that i should stay 14 days
here for the treatment of a lung infection by Pseudomonas
aeruginosa. Please do not worry. It is only an infection. But
it has to be treated right away. My kidneys, my liver,
my heart, my digestive tract all function well. I am given
two strong anti-biotics, four I.V. injections per day. And
the clinicians here are monitoring closely the process of
treatment. I am allowed to go out of the hospital to the
park nearby one hour per day to do walking meditation.

Love Letter One

Boston August 21, 2009

Dear Friends and Co-practitioners
at the Retreat <u>One Buddha is not enough</u>
Estes Park, Co.

My dear friends,

I am writing to you from the Massachusetts General Hospital in Boston. I know the Sangha has manifested in Estes Park. I miss the retreat. I miss the beautiful setting of the retreat. Especially I miss the Sangha, I miss you. I always enjoy sitting with the Sangha, walking with the Sangha, breathing with the Sangha. The joy of being together, sharing the Dharma and the Practice together is always very nourishing and healing.

But i do not suffer, because i know i am taking care of myself. And taking care of myself is to take care of you. The doctors here decided that i should stay fourteen days for the treatment of a lung infection by <u>Pseudomonas aeruginosa</u>. Please do not worry. It is only an infection. But it has to be treated right away. My kidneys, my liver, my heart, my digestive tract all function well. I am given two strong antibiotics, four I.V. injections per day. And the clinicians here are monitoring closely the process of treatment. I am allowed to go out of the hospital to the park nearby one hour per day to do walking meditation.

②

There are almost 1000 of us now practicing together at the
Estes Park Retreat. It must be joyful. I am confident
that our many Dharma teachers, lay and monastic, are
conducting the Retreat the best way we can. Dear friends,
if you look deeply enough, you will see me in the
Retreat, walking with you, sitting with you, breathing
with you. I feel clearly that i am in you and you
are in me. In this Retreat, you will witness to the
talent of the Sangha: you will see that Thây is
already well continued by the Sangha, and the Presence
of the Sangha carries Thây's presence. Please let me
walk with your strong feet, breathe with your healthy
lungs and smile with your beautiful smiles.

   We had finished a wonderful and joyful Retreat
at Stone Hill College in the State of Massachusetts before
Thây went to the Hospital for a check-up. The doctors
said that we should not delay the treatment. So Thâ
is doing his best here for you and you are doing your
best up there for Thay. In that way we can still
enjoy our true Togetherness. Please enjoy the retreat
for me, and bring home a set of the Dharma talks
given at the Stone Hill Retreat, especially the last one.
I hope to write to you again in a few days, before
the end of the Retreat. Yours faithfully,

                              Nhat Hanh

There are almost 1000 of us now practicing together at the Estes Park Retreat. It must be joyful. I am confident that our many Dharma teachers, lay and monastic, are conducting the Retreat the best way we can. Dear friends, if you look deeply enough, you will see me in the Retreat, walking with you, sitting with you, breathing with you. I feel clearly that i am in you and you are in me. In this Retreat, you will witness to the talent of the Sangha: you will see that Thay is already well continued by the Sangha, and the presence of the Sangha carries Thay's Presence. Please let me walk with your strong feet, breathe with your healthy lungs, and smile with your beautiful smiles.

We had finished a wonderful and joyful Retreat at Stone Hill College in the State of Massachusetts before Thay went to the Hospital for a check-up. The doctors said that we should not delay the treatment. So Thay is doing his best here for you and you are doing your best up there for Thay. In that way, we can still enjoy our true Togetherness. Please enjoy the retreat for me, and bring home a set of the Dharma talks given at the Stone Hill Retreat, especially the last one. I hope to write to you again in a few days, before the end of the Retreat. Yours faithfully,

Nhat Hanh

1: This Is It

Brother Phap Hai and Sister Tue Nghiem

A FAMOUS ZEN MASTER of the Sufi tradition called Mullah Nasrudin was once invited, as many Dharma teachers are, to give a series of talks at the local mosque. He was feeling, as many of us do, a little confused; he didn't know what he was going to speak about. So, on the first Friday he got up on the pulpit and said, "Brothers and sisters, how many of you know what I'm going to speak about today?" Everyone in the audience shrugged and looked at him mystified, and said, "We don't know what you're going to talk about mullah." The mullah said, "Then I'm not going to waste my time with you people. I'm leaving." So he left. When he got out the door, he thought "Safe! I'm safe, for one week; it's all good."

Then came the second week. Mullah Nasrudin got up in the pulpit and asked, "How many of you know what I'm going to speak about today?" The audience thought, "We'll play it safe," and they said, "We all know, we all know." The mullah said, "Then I don't need to say anything. Today's teaching is over." And he left, thinking, "Whew, safe again!"

Now came the real test. It was the third Friday, and the last in the series of talks. He climbed up to the pulpit and said, "Dearly beloved, how many of you know what I'm going to speak about today?" The people in the audience looked at each other. Half the audience nodded and the other half shook their heads. The mullah was very calm. He said, "Fine. The side that nodded can share with the others what I'm going to speak about. My job is done."

One day in Plum Village, Thay was sitting and giving a Dharma talk when it started to rain. Thay stopped the Dharma talk and said, "Everyone just listen to the rain; that's the real Dharma talk." We sat there in silence and listened to the rain—not only with our ears, but with our eyes, with our whole body; just sitting there present for the rain. Meditation practice is exactly that. It's learning to listen to what life is presenting to us in every moment. Meditation and mindfulness practice teach us to be open, not only with our ears, but with our eyes, with our whole body, and with our heart. Whatever is going on in our lives, no matter how busy we are, we have opportunities to practice sitting meditation, walking meditation, and eating meditation. We have so many different gifts to unwrap.

Whatever we're doing in our day we can set this intention: to be present for whatever presents itself. Meditation practice is like learning to lift up a cup and put it down, lifting it up and putting it down again and again. How do we interact with what's there for us? Do we close down, do we open up, or do we ignore it?

You may have heard the term "engaged Buddhism" to describe this kind of mindfulness practice. At its very heart, engaged Buddhism is using daily life as our practice of awakening. *U.S. News and World Report* once reported that Americans spend an average of six months of their lives waiting—waiting at the stop light, waiting in the checkout line, waiting here, waiting there. My question is, "Waiting for what?" Six months is a long time. Some of those moments are quite challenging. What are we doing during those moments? These are all potential moments of practice. We can't always choose our circumstances, but we can choose how to respond.

Some years ago, I was sitting next to Thay on the deck of the Still Sitting hut. This is Thay's hut in the Upper Hamlet of Plum Village in France. It's a very little hut and there's a deck outside overlooking the vineyards. I was a very young novice at the time, and I was so nervous sitting next to Thay. I didn't know where to look and didn't know what to do. I thought I'd better be very proper, so I just sat there. After awhile, Thay looked over to me and said, "Brother Phap Hai." I said, "Yes, Thay." He said, "If you're going to sit here, swing your legs." So…I swung my legs. But I also realized the deep teaching that Thay was giving me. In every moment, wherever we are, sitting here, let us swing our legs, let us find what we need to find in order that this moment becomes the most pleasant moment of our life.

Thay tells us that we know we're practicing correctly if we immediately feel relief; the Dharma is described as being "immediately useful and effective." In the year 2000, Thay and a number of monastics were asked to go to Australia to lead a retreat. Being monastics, we tend to choose the cheapest airline ticket possible. So going from Bordeaux to Sydney took us over forty hours. By the time we arrived in Sydney, we were exhausted. I will never forget walking up the stairs of the house where we were staying with two suitcases in my hands. They were so heavy. Each step was heavier and heavier. And when I got to my room, I put them down, and without a thought at all, I went, "Ahhhh." I just came back to my breath, my whole body relaxed, and I felt wonderful putting down those bags.

Later, I was doing sitting meditation, and I realized that that "ahhhh" is exactly what we're talking about when we speak of ahh-rriving and ahh-wareness. With every step, with every breath, with every conversation, we can put down our worries and let go of our plans and just be where we are.

Mindfulness is not a head game. We should be able to feel our arrival in our bodies, because mindfulness is the embodiment of being present. The word "mindfulness" is a translation of the word *sati* in Pali or *smrti* in Sanskrit. In the Indian psychology of the time, the seat of consciousness was not seen to be the brain, but the heart. Now we know that consciousness is in every cell of our body, not just in our head.

If we make a fist with our dominant hand, whether it's our right or left hand, with effort we can hold it maybe a minute or two. Then our tendons, muscles, and ligaments will start to be tired and painful, and it will become quite difficult to continue. You can experiment on your own if you wish. So naturally when we feel this tightness and

tension, this stress, we want to do the opposite and open our hand up completely. But if we try to maintain our hand stretched open like that, then we feel the same tightness, and the ligaments will become tired and start to shake, and eventually we'll have to release our open palm. We have to find the point of balance. In mindfulness practice we find the point in between, enjoying each moment but with that intention, with that ahh-wareness.

It is so difficult to arrive at this awareness, because there is our tendency to think, think, and think all the time. There's a constant chattering in our minds. Mindful breathing, mindful walking, and mindful eating are just different tools to help us to come back to the present moment and to be aware of what's going on.

Mindful Breathing

Everything we do can be a gentle reminder to arrive in the present moment, arrive in the here and the now, and arrive in our body. The element that helps us to arrive is the energy of mindfulness. Mindfulness means the awareness of whatever is happening inside us and around us. The energy of mindfulness is something that's innate in us; we all have that capacity to be mindful. And mindfulness is the foundation of all the practices we describe here.

When we're mindful of our body, our emotions, and what is going on around us, we're really stopping and arriving each moment. The arriving allows us to see deeply into ourselves, and to savor the life that's offered to us. When we're able to be mindful, aware, and in the moment, we're really touching the capacity of the Buddha inside of us. This is true for everyone, not just monks and nuns. Each of us can continue the Buddha, by dwelling with mindfulness in the moment and savoring every opportunity that we have to be together as a community, as a family.

The first tool that we use to stop the chattering and return to the present moment is our breath. We breathe all the time, but mindful breathing is being aware that the air is coming into our lungs and coming out. We can be aware of our abdomen rising as the air comes in, and our abdomen falling as the air goes out. Whenever we're able to be aware of our breathing, we're truly present for our body and for our life.

Let's breathe for a minute. Bring your attention to your nostrils and just feel the air coming in and the air going out; the cool air coming in, the warm air coming out. You can place your hands on your abdomen and feel the rising and the falling of the abdomen as you breathe in and as you breathe out.

You can say quietly to yourself, "Breathing in, I feel the air coming in through my nostrils. Breathing out, I feel the air going out of my nostrils. In, my abdomen is rising. Out, my abdomen is falling." You can shorten this to, "In, Out."

This is conscious breathing; it's not controlled breathing. We just acknowledge the air coming in and going out. We acknowledge that our lungs and our abdomen are expanding and deflating as we breathe in and out. We're not trying to manipulate or control our breathing, because that would only make us tired. It's about bringing awareness, mindfulness, to the breathing.

You don't have to wait for a retreat or for a particular activity to take place to practice mindful breathing. The practice is happening moment to moment. It's like stringing beads together to create a rosary. Each time we come back to our breathing, we're stringing one bead on to this long rosary. The more beads we put on, the more moments of our day are spent in awareness. All the beads add up. Little moments help the seed of mindfulness in us to grow. When the seed of mindfulness is large, then it really helps us to live our life deeply, it helps us to savor the life that is there for us. The energy of mindfulness is what makes a Buddha a Buddha. A Buddha is someone who's mindful twenty-four hours a day. We may only be part-time Buddhas, as Thay likes to say, but the mindful moments add up together to the point when we can reclaim our nature as a Buddha.

I love the image of our mind as a pond. On a day when it's rainy and cloudy, we see ripples, waves, and fragments of the landscape reflected on the pond. On a clear, still day, the water is so calm and clear that we can see the reflections of the blue sky, the clouds, and the trees in it. And our mind is like that. When we're able to practice mindful breathing, our mind becomes so clear and so calm that we can see very deeply into the roots of our being, into who we really are. It is the seeing that frees us.

Mindful Walking

Usually we're so habituated to always doing things in our life—we have this and that thing to do, this and that place to go—that we're never really there. We think that happiness and peace and whatever we're looking for are going to come to us when we get over there. We think, "Oh, if only I could close the door I'd be happy." "If only I could turn the air conditioning down just a little, everything would be perfect." "Another cup of coffee, oh, that's just what I need." So all of these things come to us and we go after them.

In our life, when we walk, we're usually walking to go somewhere. We walk out of the meditation hall in order to get somewhere. We walk to our car or to the bathroom. First, we're here, then we're over there, and then suddenly we're somewhere else and we lose the moments in between; because we're used to focusing on our destination or on what we'll be doing once we're there.

Walking meditation is one of the most beautiful practices in our tradition. With each step, we practice arriving. Thay likes to give the example of the seal and wax that people used to use on envelopes; many of us have probably seen a picture of this. You melt the wax on to the paper and then press the seal into the hot wax, making an imprint and sealing the envelope. When we practice walking medita-tion, we imprint our presence on the earth. We arrive with every step we make. If we're really there for each step, there's a good chance we will truly be there when we get to our destination.

A few years ago in Plum Village, Thay said in a Dharma talk, "You can save up your money for a long time to buy an airline ticket, reg-ister for a retreat in Plum Village, and stay there for perhaps three weeks. When you get home you can show everyone the stamp in your passport and say, 'Look, I went to Plum Village.' But if you haven't practiced walking meditation in Plum Village, you haven't truly been there at all."

In walking meditation, we breathe in as we take two, three, or four steps, depending on the length of our in-breath. As we breathe out, we can take three or four steps, depending on the length of our out-breath; and we enjoy the movement of our body, the air, and the sunshine. If we practice walking meditation, our mindfulness doesn't end as we move from one activity to another. Each activity is a continuation of the one before.

Mindful Eating

Hopefully you have the opportunity to practice eating mindfully at least three times a day. We monastics have a practice that I would like to share with you. When we get our utensils and plate or bowl, we take a moment to bow and recognize that our bowl is empty. This is not philosophical emptiness. This is the simple recognition that, at this point in time, there is nothing in the bowl, nothing on the plate, and that in a few moments we'll have the opportunity to put some-thing there. So how lucky we are. In that spirit, we take our food. We take what we need for our body, which is sometimes different from what we want. We take what we're sure we can finish.

Once we have our food, we find a place to sit down with friends in the practice. Before we eat, we give thanks to the earth, the universe, and all the hard work that went into our meal. Once we've begun our meal, we're encouraged to sit for fifteen or twenty minutes until we finish our food. There's no hurry. It's a meditation. If we practice eating meditation, many things are revealed to us. There was a brother of French origin in Plum Village who noticed that although he had the intention to chew his food thoroughly, he would put the spoonful of food in his mouth and unconsciously gulp it down. After a number of years of practicing eating meditation, a memory emerged. He was raised in Algeria just after the Second World War, at which time food was rationed. As a very young child, he'd once eaten his family's supply of bread for the day and his father had beaten him. So he had developed this tendency to gulp down his food. Slowly, over time, that memory was revealed to him and he was able to practice to transform it. Eating meditation doesn't just take place at the table. It's related to how we interact with the conditions of happiness in our life.

Listening to the Bell and Stopping

Using a mindfulness bell is another tool for stopping the chattering and helping us arrive. When we listen to the bell, we stop everything. We stop walking, we stop moving, we stop talking; we not only quiet our mouths, but we also quiet our minds, and simply come back to our breathing and our body. We take that moment to really rest and check in with how our body is doing, letting go of any tension.

A mindfulness bell doesn't have to look like a typical bell. In our community, we also use the telephone. With the first three rings of the telephone, we stop ourselves, everything we're doing, and we come back to our body and our breathing, we rest in our body, we rest in the moment. Sometimes, we use the church bell. The sound of a bird can be a mindfulness bell. The sound of the creek is also a bell of mindfulness. Listening to the bell, you can sit in any position you like, the lotus or the chrysanthemum position, so long as you sit upright, relax your shoulders, and put a light smile on your lips. And we can also use silence as a bell of mindfulness. We don't say "hit" the bell but "invite" the bell. The bell is our friend. We don't want to hit our friend, we want to invite our friend to sing. In this case, the bell will sing for us. We stop what we're doing or saying and just listen to the bell and breathe in and out.

Noble Silence

In Buddhist practice, for something or someone to be called "noble," the three aspects of its being—body, speech, and mind—need to be united. So noble silence is not just about not talking. We all know that sometimes not talking isn't noble at all, for example, when we refuse to communicate with someone. During the time of noble silence in the evening, we can practice becoming aware of the whole of our body, relaxing deeply, sending gratitude to our organs for working so hard, and relaxing all the muscles. We can also be aware of whatever we're doing. "Do I really need to do this thing right now, or am I just being busy?"

When we practice noble silence, we get a chance to rest our breath energy, the energy we use for talking, and to be aware of what's coming in, what's going out. We can ask, "Do I really need to say this thing right now?" "Am I really communicating something, or am I just filling in space?" There's an activity we sometimes do with the young adults in which they sit facing each other, just being open and looking at each other for a couple of minutes. Many of them share that it's excruciatingly intimate. We can't hide behind jokes, sarcasm, or chatting about the weather. We're just who we are. You're just who you are. This is the gift of noble silence, being who we are and allowing the other person to be who they are. We offer each other space. At the same time, the communication is very deep. Noble silence is not about cutting ourselves off, but about communicating deeply with each other. Let us greet each other with a smile, look at each other and acknowledge each other as family members. We can communicate deeply without words.

The other aspect of our being in noble silence is in our mind.

"What am I thinking about? Where am I putting my attention in this moment? On what's going wrong? On my worries, my anxieties, my plans? On what's going on at home, or what we're going to have for breakfast tomorrow morning?" All of these things go through our minds. When we practice noble silence, we practice being aware of where we're putting our attention, and bringing it back to what is nourishing to us. It brings us back to our intentions. In this way, our practice of noble silence becomes something solid, transformative, and beautiful that we can offer to each other.

Sitting Meditation

We can practice stopping and breathing at any time in our daily lives. But sometimes it's helpful to take time for just sitting and breathing. This is sitting meditation. For sitting meditation, it's good to have a cushion, or something to support our back. We sit on the edge of the cushion, helping our psoas muscle to be engaged, helping to keep our spine aligned and relaxed. If we were to sit in the middle of the cushion, we'd tend to fall backward and trying to compensate for it makes this position very tiring, and not very beautiful; we can create back pain by sitting this way for a long time. It's really important to be able to have our back in a supported position so our spine can be straight.

Our two knees should be touching the ground. One foot can be placed on top of the opposite thigh, this is what we call the half-lotus position. If our legs are flexible, we can sit in the full lotus position with each foot crossed over to rest on the opposite thigh. We can sit on a bench with our legs underneath it. If we sit on a chair, it's important to keep our back upright and our feet flat on the floor. We can put our hands wherever they feel comfortable; they might be one on top of the other in our lap, or on each knee. It's important that our posture is upright and that we feel comfortable. We can close our eyes or we can open our eyes, lowering our gaze to a place two or three feet in front of us. If we're sleepy, it's good to open our eyes so that we can be awake. If we're feeling distracted by the people around us, it's good to close our eyes so that we can concentrate better.

Once we've established our posture, we're sitting beautifully, what do we do next? We can go back to our breathing. Be aware of the in-breath and the out-breath, be aware of our lungs, our diaphragm extending and deflating as we breathe in and out. We can also be aware of our body, and bring our awareness to different parts of our body. I always like to start with my toes and my feet because when I'm with my toes and my feet, I'm as far away from my head as possible. If I start with my head, I get caught in the thinking. So it's important for me to start with my toes and my feet, and to feel the sensations there. Then we can bring our awareness up to our knees, our thighs, our back. Wherever we bring our awareness into our body, it helps that part of the body to relax, it helps the tension there to be released.

We take a moment to check in with the body, to see how our body posture is. Is it upright? Is it relaxed? Where are our hands? Are they in our lap? Are they on our knees? Are we looking down too low or is our head resting comfortably on our spine and our shoulders? We come back to our breathing, acknowledge it, and be aware of the air coming in and out. We feel the abdomen rising and falling as we breathe in and out. We bring our attention to our toes and our feet. We feel the sensations in our toes and our feet. We may also want to wiggle our toes, see how that feels. Notice that when we pay attention to our toes and our feet and the sensations there, we're also with our breathing at the same time. We notice our breathing and that every part of our body is breathing. It's not just the nose, the lungs, the diaphragm, but every cell of our body is breathing. The toes and the feet are breathing too. It's important to allow our toes and our feet to breathe. When we are able to allow our toes and our feet to breathe, we can dwell in ourselves, we can be grounded without having to think and be in our head.

If we notice that a thought pops into our mind, we just acknowledge it, smile to it, and then come back to our toes and our feet, come back to our breathing. We may want to smile softly to ourselves, smile to our body, smile at any distracting thoughts that may arise in our head. We smile to our breathing, smile to the fact that we are alive. With each in-breath and out-breath, we're smiling for ourselves, we're smiling for Thay, as Thay has asked us to smile our beautiful smile for him. We smile to the fact that we're coming together as a family like this, to create peace in ourselves, in this large family, and also for the world. And each step that we take is a sign of peace. Each breath we take is for peace.

Brother Phap Khoi

When the Dharma Teacher Council convened for the first time in Colorado, three things were on my mind: the Sangha, Thay's state of health, and the retreatants. I took a look around the room and a sense of ease gradually swept away my self-imposed anxiety. The Sangha was there. Ease enveloped the room and the community. The retreat was going to happen. The Sangha was ready. The question was whether the retreatants were ready. Would they all leave once they found out that Thay was not going to be there? Would their disappointment take over their hearts? Was their confidence in the Sangha deep enough for them to remain in the retreat until the end? Well, they answered these doubts of mine that first night in the Assembly Hall with their silence and solidarity. I don't think any one of us who was there could forget that moment. The silence. The release of mental tension, of realizing that the retreat would go on. It felt as though we were all united in mind and all loving thoughts were directed eastward toward Massachusetts General Hospital, toward Thay. That silence was so palpable, so nurturing. It was the silence that heals.

A Living Thay by Caleb Lazaro

In Colorado, time disappeared and my life began to just be. In between activities with my brothers and sisters, and in between profound naps, I felt as if days passed by and I had nowhere left to go. The communal practice of mindfulness gently held my hand as the days went by, tenderly, and re-introduced me to my true identity. I became a child again. Every step was now my first step, every breeze a new sensation, and every person around me, regardless of their background or story, became a living miracle for me to bow to, contemplate, and smile upon.

Words about a sickly Thay were on the lips of most of us during the first two days of retreat. But as our practice deepened, this notion withered away; it slowly left our thoughts, and the reality of a living Thay—within us and among us—began to fill our broken hearts.

Whatever peace, love, and compassion the monks and nuns had during these six days, they poured over us selflessly, as if we were their own blood children. The very experience of this community became Thay's presence—the spirit of relentless and compassionate love being expressed mutually, mindfully, and unconditionally wherever we turned. To hear about this is not enough. To experience it is to know that the Kingdom of God is truly at hand.

Harriet Wrye

Arriving for check-in, we realized that, among the nearly thousand pilgrims, only a few of us knew that Thay would not be there. We would hold it and breathe more deeply into our vows. "One Buddha is Not Enough." Deep within the cells of his lungs, Thay must have known all along. Well, we're here. Perfect. The shifting shapes and colored clouds in the Rocky Mountain sky are extraordinary.

Thay's love letter set our course. It rattled some and guided others. The monastics reached deep into the well and offered the most amazing, wonderful Dharma. In the end, we cooked up a skit with a panoply of voices reflecting the range of disappointment, anger, incredulity, and softening that had emerged about Thay's absence, but no one volunteered to be the voice to express the theme of deep loss that had also permeated our sharings—so I agreed. In the mostly humorous skit that resolved with the reaffirmation of the power of Sangha, I spoke about how Thay's absence triggered in all of us the old wounds, the losses and abandonments, feared and real.

That night I awoke, the moon was full, the sky cloudless, and the lines I had uttered in the skit began to penetrate much more deeply into an awakening. Lying on my bunk, thinking about the deep abandonments and losses shared in our group—lost pregnancies, divorces, heartbreaks, serious illnesses—I realized in a fresh way how much we bring to our love of and longing for Thay from our own unconscious and history.

I was flooded with my own memories of my early mother's love. Of sitting in her lap in the backseat of the car, my small face nuzzled against her soft cheek, her gentle voice soothing me to sleep. How I miss that! But how present it is in this very moment. She died in a car crash thirty years ago. And seeing in Thay the father I so wished I had—attuned, reflective, rather than the literally deaf and psychologically unavailable blustery father I did have, but who was also the smart provider-father who died 18 years ago—I felt palpably refreshed, infused with the teaching of my ancestors' presence in my whole being, and the interconnectedness of all beings great and small.

In the Eyes of the Sangha by Soren Kisiel

"Thay...will not be coming to Colorado." My friend's words were carefully chosen: neutral, to lessen the blow.

Volunteering at the Order of Interbeing sign-in table, I heard those words before most people did. Some of the Dharma teachers had been informed, and I found myself privy to their whispered conversations.

My first thought was for Thay's health. But once it had been explained to me that he was in good hands and didn't seem to be in danger, disappointment came to me in such a rush that my head swam. I thought of my wife's efforts, single parenting for a week so I could be here, and of the money I'd spent to get here. I would be ordaining in the Order of Interbeing at this retreat. But without Thay? What would that mean? Could one be ordained without Thay?

A line was forming at my registration table. "If you can't practice nonattachment here," I whispered to myself, "where can you?" I took a few breaths, found a smile, and continued signing people in.

> the morning sun
> brightens the mountainsides
> whether my heart is light or not

Thay's letter was read to us, and the monastics forged ahead with the retreat. I decided: this retreat would be all about my practice. My disappointment began to lift. I could make the best of the opportunity by practicing fervently. I was here.

Then something happened. As the monastics began to share with us—in the Dharma talk and private hellos—there was our teacher! There was Thay, right before our eyes! His teaching, his understanding, his gentleness, so carefully transmitted to our monastic brothers and sisters. We were dazzled by how diligently they'd learned, and I was filled with gratitude for their efforts. In return we all sat a little straighter, practiced a little deeper. More people practiced mindful walking after that first Dharma talk than I'd seen at any other retreat.

Within a day or so, as we became used to seeing Thay in each monk and nun, we began to look for him in every one of us. And there he was. In each person's eyes, in each smile, in each gentle step. His presence permeated the retreat. Something very precious was taking place. We all felt it. We discussed this in our Dharma discussion groups. Here was interbeing, right before our eyes. Thay and the Sangha were one and the same. We and the Sangha were one and the same. Here was Thay, present with each of us, in each of us.

Suddenly I felt lucky to be at this retreat. The Sangha was crystallizing into a glittering diamond. It was developing confidence in itself, in its strength and ability to support, to carry on. How fortunate to be here for that—to be a part of this magical and precious teaching. When I shared my feelings with Brother Phap Hai, he joked, "Oh, great. When Thay calls tonight, I'll tell him you're glad he's not here."

my brother
is listening
I can see myself in his eyes

When I first came to the practice eighteen years ago, I was living on my own in Sri Lanka, and the practice for me became wrapped in a sort of lonely romance. It wasn't something I wanted to share with others; it was my own pursuit, meaningful, intimate, and private. I practiced alone.

After more than a decade of this style, I found Thay's teaching, and it turned my practice on its head. Thay stressed Sangha, community, to a degree that I found startling. My mentor for ordination, Rowan Conrad, tells a story of first arriving at Plum Village in the late 1980s. "You think you are here to see Thay," he reports Thay saying, "but that is a misperception. You are here to see the Sangha." Once that seed was planted, Sangha became key to my practice as well, and its support took me to depths I hadn't imagined possible, teaching me that compassion is every bit as important as wisdom. My practice began to bloom, but now it's one blossom in a wide field of flowers.

without a sound
a dewdrop
has fallen into the lake

As my ordination into the Order of Interbeing approached, to my surprise I found myself feeling that Thay's absence made a sort of sense. I missed Thay that morning, and wished he were there to be a part of it. On my way to the Dharma hall, I sat on a bench to quietly thank Thay for all I was learning. In my heart I sent my ordination to Thay as a get-well gift. But as I took this step into the community, I knew the only individual that had to be there was me. Me and the Sangha. "You think you are here to ordain with

Thay," I said to myself, "but that is a misperception. You are here to ordain with the Sangha."

The Be-in celebration that evening was filled with light and love and joy. We had seen something in one another and in ourselves. The energy of our smiles filled the room to bursting. The bears in the hills, I'm quite certain, could hear our laughter.

> *dragonflies*
> *dazzled with one another*
> *—late summer in the Rockies*

The first time I wore my brown jacket at the retreat, shortly after ordination, a woman stopped me and asked me to instruct her in walking meditation. I was thrilled at the opportunity to share. After some initial guidance, we walked together. "Picture lotuses blooming in each footstep," I told her quietly, paraphrasing Thay. "You are leaving a path of lotuses behind you." She breathed deeply at the image and smiled, eyes wet. I knew in that moment she saw Thay in me. And, in that moment, I could too. Gratitude flooded through me, deep and strong. And my eyes, too, filled with tears.

Teacher by Mike D'Ambrosio

hummingbirds greet me
solid mountains touch the sky
black bear says slow down

Jan Jahner

I am a nurse and I work in the area of serious illness and end-of-life care, so I understood the need for the prolonged course of antibiotics for Thay's illness immediately, as did my husband. So while it was sad that Thay wasn't present, it also was a relief that he was getting excellent care, and would heal and be well.

The pace and feel of the retreat had a quality of deep intentionality about it; there was an acute awareness that we were holding emotional space for Thay's presence in a non-local way. I enjoyed being there with young families and young adults. Their energy brought me hope for our future.

Because I felt Thay's presence so profoundly throughout the retreat, it is easier to feel my teacher at my shoulder when things become difficult, when my mind is too busy, when I want to bring peace into every step.

a cloud
never dies

2: A Cloud Never Dies

Sister Gioi Nghiem

IN THE LOTUS SUTRA there is a story about a great herbal doctor who could cure many people, except for his own children. His children refused to take the medicine that he prescribed and they kept getting sick. He was quite disappointed. One day, he went very far away and sent a message through someone else that he was dead. His sick children took their medicine right away and were cured. A teacher not being here is the same thing in a way. Perhaps Thay is hiding away so that we can practice together like this.

When each one of us generates the energy of mindfulness, collectively we become the Buddha in one body, one huge Sangha body. In a way, it makes each one of us stronger. This is good news. There is a Vietnamese saying: "After the rain, there will be sunshine." This reminds me of an experience I had. One day a group of brothers and sisters had planned to go on a hike, but the weather was stormy and it was raining very hard. We were sitting inside, enjoying a cup of tea together. Half the group didn't want to hike. They were afraid that by the time we got up the mountain, we'd be soaked. But Sister Patience was very enthusiastic about going up the mountain, despite the storm and the rain. She said, "Why don't we just go?" So we waited a while and then began our hike. On our way up, the rain stopped, the sky cleared, and there was sunshine.

Sometimes there are difficulties or mishaps that come our way. But if we look deeply, we see that something negative can turn out to be something good. If we're able to see the good things that come, then we don't suffer as much. It gives us confidence that there is strength within us, the energy of mindfulness, compassion, and peace that can help us to embrace, heal, and overcome obstacles. The practice of mindfulness helps us to stop in the middle of a problem or difficulty so we can recognize what is there, embrace it, look deeply into it, and take good care of it. We all have this capacity.

After I'd been a nun for about a year, my sister sent me a card with a joke inside; I think I must have been practicing too seriously! A nun went into a bookstore and bought a book for $7. She gave the salesman $10, and when he didn't give her any change, she asked, "Where is my change?" The salesman replied, "Oh, I thought change is from within." We tend to laugh at this, but in our daily life, things like this happen a lot. We expect a lot of changes to come from outside, but the change actually comes from within. It's like Mahatma Gandhi said, "We are the change we want to see in the world." So we can't just expect and wait. We need to do something about it. We can nourish our happiness, and we can transform our suffering so that the change can come from within. And from that basis, we change the surroundings. Once we make change within ourselves, then we can affect our surroundings. I'm still practicing with that. Sometimes in the community I see changes that I want made, but I forget to see that this change has to come from me. If I can't change my view or drop my perception of things, then what I suffer from is not the conditions outside, but the expectations that I'm holding on to; it may be my own view of happiness that's keeping me from being happy.

Recently I was stung by an insect and my whole left hand became numb. I found out later from a sister who specializes in acupuncture that the insect had stung me at an acupuncture point used in anesthesia. I couldn't move my fingers for twenty-four hours after the sting. Since I'm left-handed, I had to start training my right hand to brush my teeth, to shave my head, to hold a spoon, and to do many other things. It was so difficult. It forced me to eat really mindfully. But now I appreciate my left hand so much more. Before that, I hadn't recognized that having a functioning left hand was an important condition for my happiness. After several days of massaging my left hand and having treatments, the numbness decreased.

When some part of our body isn't well, we tend to suffer. But if we can recognize that other parts of the body are still working well, then we don't suffer as much. In Thay's letter, he wrote, "Don't worry about me, because my kidneys and my heart and my liver and my intestines are functioning very well." So I see his deep practice of recognizing the conditions of happiness that are there; and he doesn't suffer just because the microorganisms are in his lungs. It gives me a lot of hope.

We all have habit energies. When we come to a retreat like this we have a chance to see those habit energies coming up, especially during silent meal and silent sitting. Sometimes things come up that you might not have seen before. We just need to be there, to recognize, and to embrace with our mindful breathing whatever arises. If it's too strong, like a strong emotion, then we might want to do walking meditation in the forest or lie down and do deep breathing meditation so that we can stay with these emotions and take good care of them.

When we are moving more mindfully or when we're in a quiet place, the habit energies are easier to recognize. We don't need to get to work trying to change them. We just need to be there to recognize them and embrace them with our mindful breathing. We take good care of them and, once they've calmed down, we can look deeply into them.

Recently, I was doing a lot of driving at our monastery in upstate New York, and I started to recognize a habit energy that I hadn't seen before. I get very irritated at backseat drivers! At the monastery, we use a GPS navigator. Nevertheless, I still get lost sometimes. So during my time there, I got some comments from backseat drivers. Once we were on a long drive and at a certain point, I couldn't take it anymore. I turned to my monastic sister and said, "Sister, would you please let me drive?" I was a bit irritated. That day when I got home, I started to recognize that this habit energy was transmitted from my father. He doesn't like backseat drivers either!

I remember now that whenever I visited home, my father would drive, I would sit in the backseat, and my mother would sit next to my father. From time to time, my mother would comment on my father's driving. My father didn't use the GPS. Whenever he needed to go somewhere, he'd first look at a map and memorize all the roads

he'd be going on. If he happened to make a wrong turn, my mother would say something like, "Oh, you should have turned that way." When I recognized that habit energy from my father, I felt happy. I knew my father was in me. Now I smile to him and I practice,

"Daddy, I know you are there." It makes it much easier. Otherwise, I'd be very hard on myself and wonder, "Why am I so upset?" This way, the next time I can be more mindful and more open to what is being shared. In that way, I don't suffer as much. It makes me feel lighter. If I didn't recognize this habit energy, I'd be too hard on myself and get all upset over little comments. After this realization, I was able to drive more mindfully and not so suffer so much!

Got Milk?

This morning when I took the soymilk carton out of the refrigerator, I saw it had a sign on it that said "Got Milk?" It reminded me of a story told by one of my monastic brothers. I'm not sure how much of the story is true. This brother was working in the registration office and many people were coming in asking for things and he got very annoyed. After a while, he couldn't deal with it. So he came up with this joke. And it helped him to not get too irritated.

A duck walked into a hardware store and asked, "Got milk?" The salesman replied, "We don't have any milk here; it's a hardware store, not a grocery store!" So the duck walked out. A few minutes later, it walked back in and asked, "Got milk?" The salesman said, "I told you already, there's no milk here." The duck left and returned about half an hour later. "Got milk?" he asked. This time the salesman got angry, "How many times do I have to tell you? If you ask for milk one more time, I'm going to nail you down!" The duck looked all around the store. Then he looked back at the salesman and asked, "Got nails?" The salesman was so furious that he forgot he was in a hardware store and he said, "No, I don't have any nails." And the duck said, "Got milk?"

In our lives, there are times we feel at ease because we feel understood by the people around us. But there are moments when we feel that people just don't have enough common sense. As in the case of the duck and the salesman, we get easily irritated. When we can recognize this, we see we're more likely to be irritated by our habit energies than by the other person. With the practice of deep listening and looking deeply we can overcome our suffering. We can learn to understand ourselves, to discover what our strengths and weaknesses are so we can understand and embrace ourselves and the people around us.

In our community, we have a practice called Shining Light. We sit together and share about each other, our strengths and weaknesses. Sitting in such a circle, we have a chance to learn about our monastic brothers and sisters and about ourselves. We can look deeper into ourselves and see what energies are at work, and we embrace what we find. The practice is not about doing. We don't come to a retreat to try so hard to be concentrated, to be mindful all the time. We don't have to work at anything. We just come together to be with nature, with each other, and with ourselves. That's all it takes to go through the process of transformation and healing.

S H A R I N G S

The Buddha of the Future by Trish Nelson

In 2007, in the Rocky Mountains of Colorado, Thich Nhat Hanh quoted Master Linji: "Don't come to me for your enlightenment!" I was a little stunned to hear him say that. You can imagine how I felt at the Colorado retreat two years later when he was not there at all. Thich Nhat Hanh is made of non–Thich Nhat Hanh elements. This is the teaching of nonself, and we all got to practice it at the Colorado retreat—like kids who had just lost the training wheels from their bikes and didn't know if they were going to wipe out or keep flying down the hill. Nonself means a flower could not be without the sunshine, the water, the earth. Likewise, Thich Nhat Hanh could not be without his students, the practice, the community that supports the practice, or the beautiful earth that is always nurturing the practice through her beauty and freshness.

Facing the absence of our teacher, who is in his eighties, helped prepare us for what it will be like when his form passes. We have been told by him, "All forms are impermanent." Yes, but don't leave us! We saw together that although all forms are impermanent, the seed of awakening is in every one of us. And just as we carry our blood ancestors in our DNA, we also carry our spiritual teacher in our heart.

It has been said that the Buddha of the future, Maitreya, is not an individual but a community. If so, it is certainly a community of people practicing to live in the present, transform their own suffering, and help awaken others. It is a community of people who care about each other. Letting their own light shine, and being a light unto themselves, they also make light for the rest of the world.

Haven Tobias

Every morning in Norman, Oklahoma, I walk with Thay. Matching my steps to my breaths: "Here/now. Walking/breathing. Happy feet/peaceful steps." In the past few years, I've added to a daily outdoor walking practice of forty-five minutes, my daily sitting practice. Every morning at the same time, I cover the same ground, and it is always the same and always different. The one constant is that always Thay is with me. Walking, breathing.

I am reasonably certain Thay has never been to Norman, Oklahoma. So in Estes Park in 2009, perhaps it was easier for me than for people newer to the practice to understand that of course Thay was walking with us there. What I didn't understand was what an extraordinary experience was in store for us. It just took patience and being there fully present to watch the wonder of the Sangha unfold. We were not just walking with Thay. We were laughing with each other and offering compassion and understanding to each other and supporting each other in all the ways Thay teaches us to do and to be.

I have heard Thay say the next Buddha will be the Sangha. In Estes Park, the Sangha was the Buddha. On a conventional level, Thay was missed and we were all concerned about him. But in another dimension, we knew as a Sangha we were Thay, and he was well, and we were well, and it was enough. Thank you dear brothers and dear sisters and dear friends.

Kay Tiffany

When we first heard the announcement that Thay was ill and would not be with us, concern and worry for Thay swept through the assembled throng. But that was followed by disappointment and confusion as we grappled with the realization that we wouldn't get our infusion of inspiration and wisdom from that soft and certain voice; our teacher would not be there to lead and to feed us.

What happened instead was remarkable. Instead of just basking in the presence of Thay, everyone there became invested in working individually and together to practice the teachings. People demonstrated that the teachings can and will continue without Thay's physical presence.

A Lamp Unto Yourself by Natascha Bruckner

"Make of yourself a light / said the Buddha /
before he died."
—Mary Oliver

In truth, Thay is never absent; he always exists in some form. So in Colorado, besides grief, I am experiencing another strong feeling. It is a powerful sense of Thay's presence in me. His being is wakefulness, and it exists not only in his physical form, but in many other forms too. As Thay's students, we contain wakefulness. With our being, we carry on his purpose, which is Being itself. All Sangha members are emissaries, vehicles, for Being.

Now that he is absent, we have a chance to practice more fiercely, with sharper focus and deeper compassion. It is time to find and become the Buddha within ourselves. No one can do it for us. Awakening can't be externalized. We must abandon the hope that Thay, or anyone else, will hand it to us, or be it for us. It's up to us. It's up to me.

I imagine Thay was in this position, too, when his teacher passed away. The Buddha's students were in this position when their teacher left his form. I remember reading the Buddha's last words to his disciples: "Be a lamp unto yourself." Today each of us is faced with a choice. We may see the absence of our teacher as a form of darkness. Or we may realize our own nature of illuminating light. There we were, nine hundred strong, transforming into lamps. With so many lamps alight, the face of the earth will be beautifully illuminated.

Jessica Vanlandingham

Before the retreat, I was looking forward to receiving the special kind of learning that comes from witnessing others who are more established on the path. I wanted to enjoy the songs, in person, which I had been learning and healing with over the past six months.

As I sat in the Great Hall on the first evening, the room was softly lit. I felt stable and warm. I enjoyed knowing I was there. I enjoyed knowing I wasn't waiting. I was there in the present moment, to nourish the present moment. I enjoyed sitting, feeling stable and safe. As other people arrived to find seats, I felt happy and connected to them; they were also there to nourish our seeds of peace.

The people finding seats around me were arriving with relatively free and clear minds—it showed in their bodies and movements. They were not arriving with hurry or worry or greed. When the monastics, in simple brown robes, stood before us on the stage and sang the music that had been deeply healing for me over the last months, I noticed my sorrow.

I'd never met Thay. But when the information was shared that Thay would not be with us in his body, I did not feel the least bit shocked or disturbed. I had deep trust in the Dharma and in those teaching it. I had deep faith in my ability to practice arriving home to myself. I had come for the nourishment that comes from a community that practices and lives this!

How good that the retreat organizers had offered me peace by not giving me the information beforehand. How kind of them to allow us to arrive with joy and enthusiasm. I'm really so happy they took care of me, so that I didn't have the choice of going into discriminative thinking about whether or not to attend!

Being in that room, gathered together with over nine hundred people, how wonderful! I thought we were nothing other than a continuation of our teacher, the historical Buddha, Gautama. I was reminded of how many sutras begin by saying that the Lord was at such and such a location and that there he addressed a great community of monks and a great community of bodhisattvas. Thinking about this brought much gratitude to my mind. I thought about all the beings in each generation who have had the deep aspiration to end suffering. And their kindness has offered me a path.

One day, as I walked on a path at the retreat grounds, I saw a group of monastic brothers walking together. As I passed them, a voice in my mind commented, "It looks like those brothers have no worries." It was really a wonderful thing to catch with awareness. It woke me up to life in the moment. I saw how conditioning could have used that comment to perpetuate my absence from the now, or to keep me believing that happiness and being worry-free was not for me. I allowed another thought to be considered, "I can practice 'no worries' too! Right in this very now!" And I did. It was wonderful.

I witness others, and I am reminded of my aim. I witness others practicing and I receive nourishment.

The Truth of the Heart by Barbara Hawk

The first night in Colorado, the nuns and monks began chanting. Some were calm and smiling and chanting. Some were calm and chanting with tears streaming down their faces. Those minutes of chanting were one of the most profound Dharma teachings I have ever encountered. To see the truth of the heart, so totally held in the practice, burst a few of the restraining ties around my heart-mind. In those moments, I was reminded of Thay's teaching: "You cannot be a practitioner and not do the practice."

Aware of my inner turmoil about the "right" response to this news, I experienced a new level of compassion, a deeper willingness to just hold the feelings and continue breathing in, breathing out. Breathing with the monks and nuns in gratitude, breathing to offer solidity, breathing to offer love and respect and support to them and to Thay, breathing to the "this-is-what-is" of it all. In those moments, I understood, I experienced the monks and nuns as Thay's continuation. I understood in a new way myself as Thay's continuation and all of us as Thay's continuation.

3: No Mud, No Lotus

Brother Phap Nguyen (Dharma Source)

I'D LIKE TO BEGIN my sharing by reading a poem to you. This poem is from one of my dear spiritual ancestors, an American spiritual ancestor. You might be familiar with him.

> *Two roads diverged in a yellow wood,*
> *I'm sorry I could not travel both*
> *And be one traveler, long I stood*
> *And looked down one as far as I could*
> *To where it bent in the undergrowth;*
>
> *Then took the other, as just as fair,*
> *And having perhaps the better claim*
> *Because it was grassy and wanted wear;*
> *Though as for that the passing there*
> *Had worn them really about the same,*
>
> *And both that morning equally lay*
> *In leaves no step had trodden black.*
> *Oh, I kept the first for another day!*
> *Yet knowing how way leads on to way*
> *I doubted if I should ever come back.*
>
> *I should be telling this with a sigh*
> *Somewhere ages and ages hence:*

Two roads diverged in a wood, and I,
I took the one less traveled by,
And that has made all the difference.

That's from our dear spiritual teacher Robert Frost, written in 1914 or 1915, published in his book *Mountain Interval.* If you went through the American school system, you may have heard that poem quite a bit. I did. But it wasn't until I took a leap into monastic life, becoming a part-time Buddha and full-time practitioner as a monk, that this poem began to have a different meaning. Before, this poem seemed regretful, but after about two weeks of being a monk, when I had the wonderful opportunity of being Thay's attendant, this poem started to seem like a celebration of nonattachment.

I was with Thay in his hut in Plum Village. When it was time to go to the Dharma hall with Thay, I was nervous. My job was to hold Thay's bag that contained his notes and his thermos. Thay stepped out of his hut and looked at me, his eyes full of compassion. It wasn't a scary look, although sometimes Thay's compassionate look can be scarier than a scary look! His look seemed to say, "My poor child, why do you stretch yourself out so?" Then he smiled, took my hand, and took my elder brother's hand, and said, "My dear child, are you ready to go to the Pure Land?" The Pure Land is the ultimate dimension. I was surprised. "Yes, Thay, sure," I said.

Whenever Thay asks a question, you always say "yes" even if you're not sure. Thay gently took my arm as though I was a little child. Something beautiful about Thay is his combination of being a very, very wise person and also being like a child at the same time. He can switch back and forth and manifest one or the other or both. At that moment he had a boyish look on his face, he swung our arms and said "One, two, three, let's go!"

This was a little bit like what we call "Zen shock-therapy," when someone or something pulls you out of where you're caught. We suffer because we hold on to something, like clenching our fist. In this case, Thay was trying to wake me up from my own fear, from

my own expectation, from my own nervousness; opening me up to release me from myself. But he was also using a Buddhist figure of speech to ask me a deep question, "Are you ready to really live? Are you ready to face yourself and embrace yourself? Are you ready to seize your life?" This is what I took from those words.

Looking Deeply

Are you ready to grow wings and soar? Are you ready to enter the Pure Land? One, two, three, let's go. The first step of the path is to cultivate the intention to be aware. And this cultivating of the intention is something that we come back to time and time again. We come back to the intention to take the leap. The next question to ask is, "What is holding me back?" "Why can't I fly?" "Why can't I enter the Pure Land?" "Why can't I live?" To answer these questions we need to practice looking deeply to discover what habit energies and conditioned responses are holding us back. As practitioners of meditation, we learn that a very big part of what is holding us back is our habits, what we call *vasana*, our conditioned responses.

Ever since I was very young, one of the reasons I've loved the Dharma is because it helps me learn how to love. We all have the intention to love, to bring goodness and lightness to those we care about, to the world around us, to our community, our workplace, our partner. I dearly want to love my brothers and sisters. Sometimes it's easy. But sometimes it's a practice, and no matter how hard I try, I fall prey to my own habitual traps. Have you ever found yourself waking up every morning with the same old song in your head? The old song kept playing over and over for me. Even when people and circumstances changed, I'd relive the same drama. Now, I am finally learning how to stop.

Stopping can be done through sitting or walking meditation or just listening to the bell. I think of stopping as actually a bit of stretching. We use mindfulness to massage our heart and allow it to relax, release, and open a little wider. When we stretch our heart, we don't stretch it out of shape; instead we exercise it and allow it to gain flexibility and strength, just as we do with our muscles. If we practice looking deeply without expanding our heart, then we tend to get injured.

When I was a novice monk, I was close to a number of brothers; we loved each other and drove each other crazy at the same time. We all had ideas about how we should practice mindfulness and that the other monastics had it all wrong. I'd think, "I can't wait for another year or two so I can get sent to another hamlet." "Hamlets" are what we call the different monasteries of Plum Village. From time to time the brothers and sisters rotate to bring some fresh air to a different monastery.

I'd think, "Maybe in a year I'll get the chance to switch hamlets and be with people who really practice." That day eventually came. I switched hamlets but even though the brother I argued with was no longer living with me, I found a replacement for him. We argued about the same things, and the things that drove me crazy about the new brother were the same things that had driven me crazy about the other brother. I had to practice stopping and looking deeply or I was going to keep finding that same brother wherever I went.

The way to break free from our habits and our conditioning is the two-fold training of *shamatha*, stopping, and *vipashyana*, looking deeply. We can carry this two-fold training with us throughout our life: in our sitting meditation, walking meditation, eating meditation, in our watching the stars or the sunrise meditation. We can stop and allow our mind and heart to rest and relax. Sometimes our heart and mind are wound up so tight. We can massage our heart and allow it to relax, release, and open a little wider. We stretch our heart. We don't stretch it out of shape. Just as before any physical endeavor, like walking in the Rocky Mountains, or before you do an hour or two of sitting meditation, it's helpful to stretch our body.

It's essential in terms of our meditation practice to touch that stillness, that spaciousness, that relaxing of our body and our mind before we're able to practice our second aspect of the training, vipasyana, looking deeply. If we practice vipasyana without stretching our heart, then we can easily stand to get injured. If we don't stretch our heart, we tend to use our head a bit too much and over-analyze, which doesn't really get us very far. So in all our meditation practices, cultivating that aspect of stillness is something that we do and it grows and strengthens just like our muscles grow when we exercise.

When we first begin the practice, it may be very difficult to touch that stillness. Sometimes we push ourselves very hard as practitioners. Americans have a very strict ideal of perfection. We find the Dharma, we read a wonderful book by Thay or another teacher, and we think, "Okay, I've found the path, I'm going to practice, and I'm going to fix myself." And then we come to the retreat. We look around, and everybody else looks so peaceful and I feel like I am a mess. But I know this is a conditioned response, this is something that I've inherited from our American psyche: "I've gotta do it right, gotta be the best, gotta be the perfect practitioner."

We need to let go of all that. That's the beginning of our stopping, our releasing, our relaxing, our opening and stretching our heart. We need to give ourselves time and space. After such a long time of traveling at warp speed, at the speed of life, we can't just hit the brakes. So we practice cultivating slowing down. We don't stop right away. We know we have the capacity to be stable like the mountain, to be clear like the still lake. But maybe at this time my lake is more like a puddle, and that's okay. As we practice touching stillness with our footsteps, our sitting, with all our activities, our faculty of stillness develops. And when our mind and heart are still and relaxed, we can see things more clearly. With just a small degree of stillness, things become apparent, you don't have to strain yourself to see. We learn how to dwell with what is there outside of us and within us. There's so much that's right in front of us, but when we're distracted by so much mental noise, we can't hear it, we can't see it; we don't see the full picture.

To look deeply, we need to let go of all that. Letting go is the beginning of expanding our heart. Once our heart is open and relaxed, we can see more deeply, using more than our eyes. If we only use our eyes, we tend to strain or focus on the details. This is harmful for our eyes. To see clearly and look deeply, we need to learn how to relax our eyes. I remember coming home after being at a mindfulness retreat. This was before I was a monk. I'd been in a beautiful environment with loving people and had practiced stopping and looking deeply for five days. Walking from the front yard to the doorway, I saw some bushes with yellow flowers that I hadn't noticed before. After I unpacked, I asked my mother when she'd planted those bushes. She looked at me and told me they'd been there since we'd bought the house, years before. Sometimes we don't notice the things that are right there in front of us. As you continue on your path of practice, things become apparent to you and you can see things without trying to control them, fix them, or find an answer. We can see a wider perspective, and so we're less caught in our own habitual ways of reacting, and our understanding deepens.

On September 11, 2001, I was with other monastics in Northern California, on our way to hold days of mindfulness and a monastic retreat. Upon hearing the news, the young American monastics in particular felt we needed to do something right away. After a bit we went to ask our teacher for permission, and also for some guidance. What he shared with us shocked us. He said, "Don't do anything.

Right now, you need to take care of yourself. You're in no condition to do anything right now." So we scheduled some time for us to sit and to practice walking meditation. I think we even scheduled a beach trip, just to touch the stillness, the strength of nature, of each other, and to re-root ourselves, reconnect ourselves with that. After-ward, I think we all realized that was the wisest thing to do. And before Thay's public talk in Berkeley, the Sangha was able to offer a very peaceful energy through a ceremony and through our presence with our teacher onstage. This was something we wouldn't have been able to offer if we hadn't come back to take care of ourselves. We were very lucky to have our teacher to remind us that the wisest thing to do is not to react from that feeling of urgency, from fear, from worry, but to allow ourselves the time to be able to respond from that still point.

One way to practice looking deeply is to visualize looking at yourself and the world around you through Buddha eyes. You can imagine breathing and walking and sitting with the Buddha. If the Buddha is with us, we don't have to take everything on ourselves. The Buddha is there with us, looking through our eyes. Another practice that helps us dwell peacefully with things as they are is to allow the Buddha to breathe, to sit, to walk for us, to see that we and the Buddha are sitting and breathing together, and that we don't have to hold the responsibility by ourselves. We have all the Buddhas sitting with us, breathing with us, and helping us to transform. This is a way of looking deeply.

Another practice of looking deeply is to see each person as if only by relying on them, only with their aid can we wake up and grow to be who we really are. This was recommended by Shantideva. It is a training of stopping, looking, and listening to the other person and acknowledging their presence, their precious presence that is there right in front of us, and to take a moment to be there for those around us.

Another way of saying "looking with Buddha eyes" is "looking with the eyes of a child." Instead of looking with a fixed idea, we can play with what we see. The other day, I watched the sunset. For a few minutes, I was looking directly at the sun; this is my normal way of looking. After some time, I rooted myself, immersed myself in the stillness, and was able to look more deeply. I began to appreciate the play of the light on the rock faces of the cliffs and how they were transforming as the sun set. It was even more beautiful than looking directly at the sun. We train ourselves to see differently, to touch the beauty in many things. This helps to create more space in our mind.

Looking at Our Hand

One exercise for looking deeply is to hold up one of our hands before our eyes. When we look at our hand, we notice its shapes, lines, and creases. Now we contemplate things we enjoy doing with our hands, such as cooking, writing in our journal, composing poetry, building something, or holding the hand of a loved one. We can be grateful to our hands for all these things. As we look at our hand, I invite us to see all other hands in our hand. Looking deeply, we can see that everything we enjoy doing with our hands was passed on to us from our father, our mother, our grandparents, our family, or our spiritual teachers. All the love and understanding that we're able to express with our hands is a very precious transmission from our ancestors. This hand that we hold before us is our hand partially, but it also belongs to many other people. It is the continuation of all the hands that have come before us.

The same is true for our whole body. This way of looking allows us to transform our blaming mind. Sometimes when we suffer, we blame ourselves. We carry a heavy load of sadness and suffering, and we think the baggage is ours and that we have to carry it by ourselves. We think it's our own fault. But all the weight that we feel in our shoulders and our hearts is not our fault or anybody's fault. It's something that's been passed on, just as the wisdom and the love that we carry has been passed on.

The emotions and behavior of human beings are contagious. If we're sitting next to someone who is peaceful, their peace will gradually permeate our whole being. Similarly, if we're carrying the stress of generations, that also will be passed to those around us. Realizing that our burdens don't originate with us makes them lighter. We don't have to hold them by ourselves; our ancestors will help us. And if we practice with others, our community, our Sangha can help us, too, to carry our baggage until we're ready to put it down.

S H A R I N G S

Ann Clark

Because I am a single mom of eleven-year-old twins, I'd never been to an overnight retreat before. When I first read that Thich Nhat Hanh would be doing a U.S. retreat in Estes Park, I knew I had to go. Estes Park is one of my favorite places to escape and let my thoughts unfold. Of course, my thoughts went back to my children. I'd asked Joan Halifax if his retreat would be a good experience for my children or if it would be geared more toward adults. I didn't want my kids to have to suffer for six days so that I could have a pleasant experience. She replied simply, "Kids love his program; they will be fine. Enjoy it." That was all I needed as encouragement to go.

Part of me was nervous and didn't know what to expect. Most of me was excited. We arrived early the day of sign-in, got our room, and settled in. I dropped the kids off at the children's orientation and headed down the path to the meeting hall.

When I heard that he would not be there, I instantly wanted to cry. I was very sad about his state of health, but I mostly thought about me. The thoughts started to circle: "I paid so much money on a single mother's salary to come." "I still don't know how I'll catch up on bills after paying for this." "I took a week off of work, which I can't afford, but I did it so I could see him, and he is not here." "It is just not going to be insightful for me now." "I won't learn; it will be no different than simply listening to weekly talks at my local Zen center where I can go without having to miss work."

Very heartless and selfish thinking. Very human thinking.

I think I blocked out most of what was said after the initial reading of the letter. I saw people around me actually crying. I felt like it, but held it in. I heard people talking about trying to get their money back, leaving. I let those thoughts run through my mind as well. I walked up to the children's meeting place to pick my kids up and as we were making our trek back to our room, I told them I had some really bad news. I told them that Thay would not be attending the retreat, he was sick and in the hospital. I said I was really disappointed and sad, because I so wanted to be in his presence, so wanted them to be as well. My eleven-year-old son, Jerek, turned to me and said, "I don't care if he comes here or not, I just really hope that he is okay."

The sadness and disappointment at that very moment truly lifted, and permanently. I realized just how selfish I was being, I realized I had gone there for the wrong reason; it wasn't to learn or to better my practice, it was because I had put a man on a pedestal and hoped that being near him would somehow make me an enlightened being. I had forgotten that I've had the Buddha in me the whole time. I'd falsely assumed I could get that from him. For a period of time, I'd lost my way.

Mornings started out with a beautiful Dharma talk aimed mostly toward the children for the first hour. Then they would head up to their program and the last hour was for us big kids. Children are treated so well there, always having a spot in the front few rows with their parents so they can focus on the teachers and get something from the talk. I think I got more out of the children's part of the talks than the latter part.

My daughter, Jurnee, so enjoyed all of the wildlife that she saw running free around us, and the beauty of the mountains and flowers. She is very in tune with animals and loves beautiful scenery, so she took in as much of it as she could each day. Both children were perfectly still during silent meals, and they shared with me later about learning mindful eating skills in their children's group. I enjoyed this reflection and appreciation of our meals with them tremendously, as did they.

On the second to last day, I walked into the children's group to pick up my kids, and Jerek was on the floor talking with Brother Bernard; it looked like a pretty serious talk. After they talked for a moment together, they came over and Brother Bernard told me that Jerek wanted to receive the Five Mindfulness Trainings, not the Two Promises. He had read each of the Five Mindfulness Trainings intently, understood them fully, understood he would have to get there by 6:00 A.M. for the ceremony, knew how to do the bowing, was perfectly content with all of it, and was pretty adamant about receiving them. Brother Bernard told me that children don't typically do this, but if Jerek was that set on it, he would allow it. It was a very special moment for me to be able to receive the Five Mindfulness Trainings beside my son. And it will be wonderful to be sharing that as we continue on that path.

Jurnee received the Two Promises later that afternoon, and that was beautiful as well. They talked of having a yearly retreat, so we are already planning our next trip there. We now have a new summer vacation destination, one where we spend six days without newspapers, television, video games, Internet, work, or worry. I have two children who are more excited about that than they would be if we were to plan a trip to Disneyland. It is a beautiful thing.

David Nelson

I was tired of feeling out of sorts for some time. So, with a dear friend, I set out from California for Colorado on Highway 50, the loneliest road in the U.S. High in the Rocky Mountains I hoped to find my doctor, a teacher, to get the diagnosis and effective treatment I dearly needed. It was time to get the healing I'd been offered in the past in many places: the U.S., France, the Netherlands, and Vietnam. Each time I had benefited for a while, but slowly symptoms returned as I became forgetful and lost the good effect.

We drove from a foggy coast through vast valleys, mountains, high desert plains, then into higher alpine country.... We traversed from caffeinated coffee frenzies to gentle herbal tea moments.... We traveled for several days, experiencing road rage to no rage, then on to relaxed, peaceful cruising below the speed limit.

Upon arriving at the Estes Park YMCA with its 8,000-foot elevation, the sun felt so close and hot. Expectations were high as we first congregated in the hall for an orientation explaining how to live together for the next five days. When we found out that Thay would not attend his own retreat, huge thunderclouds formed and then opened up on to us. Downpours came not just from the sky, but from our eyes. How would he heal? How would we? Should we stay or go?

In our teacher's illness, he demonstrated a model of well-being. Even with a lung infection: "Remember to breathe."

"There are already more than enough conditions of happiness present." "Look deeply for the source of ill-being." Make a personal diagnosis and taste the truth cultivated with mindful awareness, concentration, and insight. As our teacher responsibly accepted his diagnosis and received a full course of antibiotics, monastic friends offered insightful talks and lessons with words of joy, hope, and healing. We experienced Thay through his continuation, his students.

Perhaps it was the thin, high-altitude air that also enhanced my awareness of breathing. Breathing in is noticeably a little more difficult; breathing out I smile, remembering I'm alive. I'm no longer a patient without a diagnosis. My diagnosis: "ill-being addict" or IBA. I'm captivated by my own suffering in a sad, codependent relationship. It hurts so much but I don't let it go. With this new insight I feel good about taking the mindful medicine: to be more happy, loving, and accepting of myself and others; to really see the brilliant mountain sunrise of each new day as a mindfulness bell; to pay attention to my in- and out-breaths.

Just before driving off, I'm told that Thay is recovering from his infection and that he should be present at the California retreat. I wonder, is my healing helping the teacher? Perhaps, such is the nature of interbeing. Student and teacher, water and wave, song and bird, the one in the all, and the all in the one. One Buddha Is Not Enough was instructed and experienced. With a sound of the bell I encounter "no separate self," at least for the moment. Then an idea pops up: it would be touching to see Thay at Deer Park Monastery. Breathing in I recognize that a thought about the future has manifested. Breathing out, I'm back in the mountains. In Colorado, the miracle of mindfulness is recognizing that the time is now. What a wonderful thing to learn, again, fresh in this present moment.

The Flute and My Sister the Bell
by Marc Potter

It is early morning. I am walking from my room to the assembly hall. I am stopped by the beauty of the mountains and clouds. I pause, really enjoying the present moment, then I hear the most beautiful melody being played on a wooden flute. I am standing there in the moment. Then my monkey mind says, "I wish I could play the flute. It must take years of practice. Maybe I could learn to play just that one tune. I could buy a flute. I could take a class." Then I see my dear sister stopping, listening to the flute. My sister is like a clear bell in her silence. She smiles to me. I smile to her. She brings me back to the moment, the mountain, and the melody. I am the flute. The one who plays is also the one who is played. I am the moment and the melody.

breathe
it'll be okay

4: Breathe, It'll Be Okay

Brother Phap Dung

M Y FAMILY came to live in the U.S. when I was eight or nine years old. When I was little, I grew up in Vietnam. We lived next to a big river. Below our house was a boat dock. My friends and I used to climb down there and pretend it was our hiding place. There were no parents, no adults who knew this place, and we'd just have adventures under this dock. Many young people love to have places like that, which seem to be their own world. We'd watch the fish; there were many wonderful fish. There was a pole in the water, and the little fish liked to swim around the pole. I grew up in the city of Da Nang, but because it was on a river there were elements of nature as well.

I was living there in the time right after the Vietnam War. Sometimes we had to run very quickly out of our house because someone had thrown a grenade inside. My grandma would wet a towel and put it over our mouths when we ran outside. Many families, many young children, lived in an environment that was quite frightening. Once in a while my father would put me on the front of his motorcycle and he'd take me far, far away to a beach; they have beautiful beaches there. My dad loved to ride his motorcycle along the beach. I remember the long roads and the long stretches of beach. These were memories I grew up with, so they're still in me.

I remember our journey to escape from Vietnam when I was a young boy. First we were taken to a little shack. We knew something was happening because several weeks before I remember putting all our toys in a box and having to give them away. I had a tricycle that I gave away to my friend who lived nearby. So I knew something was happening but I didn't know what. I thought we must be going somewhere far away, because each of us—my dad, my mom, me, everybody—could only take a little sack. I remember that my grandma sewed little things into our clothes. Now my family tells me it was gold. Since we couldn't take any money with us, my grandma made these little gold things and slipped them into our clothing so that wherever we ended up, we would survive at least for a while.

We sneaked into the hut and waited there. It was very dark. All of a sudden someone came and said in a whisper: "C'mon, let's go, let's go." We walked through a marsh with trees and we got very wet. Then we got into a little boat and went out to sea. The sea was full of waves. We had to go against the waves, and I remember the sound as each wave crashed against the boat until we met another boat. I was lifted onto the other boat. One of my strongest memories of being a child at that time is being lifted a lot and moved around, and just doing whatever my parents or my grandma told me to do. There's a strong image I remember from the boat ride—I don't know if it's a memory or a dream. I remember looking deep into the ocean and seeing something glaring back at me. Now I think maybe it was just the sun glinting off a can, but maybe not. As a child you form memories like that. You can't quite make out what they are, but they really stay with you.

We were all crowded tightly together on the boat; you could smell everyone. I stayed curled up with my grandma. We had very little food and we shared everything. I remember at one time all these fishes jumped onto our boat. At first, people were catching the fish and putting them in their bags, but then the captain of the boat stood up and said, "Nobody eat the fish. Everyone put the fish back." I found out later they were flying fishes. They're long and they have wings; they look like dragonflies, very beautiful. I remember one of the fish flickering in front of me, and I saw that it wanted to live. The adults would catch the fish and throw them back. I learned later from my parents that while we were traveling there was a small altar on the boat where the adults prayed, and they tried to keep incense burning there all the time. While people are praying for help, they should not kill anything. You must keep your purity when you are in need.

We ended up on an island. And then we were rescued by a huge ship. I was lifted again from one pair of hands to another. I remember this big man. I don't remember exactly what he looked like but I remember his hat. I remember he held me in his arms and he gave me an apple. The apple was huge in my mind, maybe because I was very happy. We were very hungry. We probably had enough food, but we were rationing and could only eat a little bit at a time.

We ended up at a small refugee camp in Hong Kong on the island of Macao. We didn't go to school; we invented games. I remember playing around the island. It was kind of like Robinson Crusoe. There we lived in a little shack with tin walls. We weren't allowed to throw rocks at the shack when we were playing because it made

a loud noise. I still remember some of the rules we had to follow there.

Later on, our family was invited to America, to Washington State, through a church program that sponsored families to come to the United States. When we first arrived we were taken to a two-story house. We went inside and they told us, "You will live here." There were so many rooms—one room had lots of toys. In Vietnamese villages, houses have no hallways, no separate rooms. There's just one room. At night, you just roll out your bedding and you sleep. That's what we were used to doing. I didn't want to sleep in a big room with just my brothers, so we all gathered in one room and slept on one bed.

Once I was here, I grew up just like you. I went to school. The kids made fun of me a lot. They said I was too short, I was this, I was that, and my eyes didn't look right. I had to find special kinds of friends that could relate to me. I got in a lot trouble. I didn't know how to practice back then, so I would fight back. I suffered a lot too because our family was having difficulties. They were having a hard time adjusting to being in the U.S. It was hard for them to find jobs

and hard to adapt. My mom's first job was as a janitor working in the back of a restaurant. My father found work putting watch faces together. They had to put in a lot of hours; it was very stressful for my parents, so they'd argue a lot, even after we got home from school. As kids we didn't know what to do with that kind of energy so we also sort of picked on each other. So I grew up with lots of difficulties in my heart. As a teenager, I was not very happy and I got upset very easily; I was easily agitated, easily irritated. Whenever my mother said something I would argue back. If she said "blue," I'd say "red." She'd say it's rainy, I'd say it's sunny. I was easily agitated. I liked to study, but I wasn't happy with myself.

My mother took me to a talk given by Thay because I had a lot of anger. Thay was the only Vietnamese monk who spoke English. I didn't understand Vietnamese, and I didn't have many Vietnamese friends. My mother heard about this Vietnamese monk who could speak English, so my mother took us to see him. It was in a big hall. I remember sitting there, not very excited. And I remember someone walking across the stage sooo slooooowly. The first time you see it, it catches your attention. Everyone else is acting normally, trying to find their seats. So it caught my eye and I remember it very clearly. No one was on stage, there was no banner, nothing, just a podium and a bell. A monk came onstage and sat down and invited the bell, and the whole atmosphere in the room changed. I remember that experience. That was the first time I'd ever seen anything like that.

My mom had taken us to the temple every Sunday, but this was the first time I'd ever experienced that change in the atmosphere of a place. That energy interested me and I became very curious about it. Several years later my mom took me to my first retreat with the monks and nuns and with Thay. As a young adult I became very interested in meditation and started learning about it.

I started to sit at home. Our home had an altar room, or a breathing room. Each Asian home has an area in the house where we put an altar. We had an ancestors' altar with a picture of my grandfather, my grandmother, and all of our ancestors who've passed away. On top was a picture of the Buddha. And on the bottom there was a Buddha of the Earth from my grandmother's tradition of ancestral worship. She's from an old Chinese tradition. So we had three areas. It's kind of like the breathing room that Thay talks about. I remember as a young boy going there, and about twice a year we would cook all kinds of wonderful food to offer on the altar. We would offer incense and invite our ancestors to come and eat with us. It was a way of celebrating their life. I remember being taught by my grandma that if

you got A's in school or something wonderful happened, you could communicate with your ancestors through this altar. In our family, you can go to the ancestral altar and light incense to announce your success to your ancestors and to thank them for helping. We moved a lot, but everywhere we went, we always had that altar, whether it was in a corner or in a room, it was always part of our life. Once in a while, on a full moon evening, my grandma and I would sit and fold papers that we would send to our ancestors. This is also from my grandma's tradition. She lived as though her ancestors were still alive and you could send them things, just like sending them a fax and saying, "We're okay down here." I remember when I'd burn these paper prayers, or sometimes paper money, she'd say the higher the ash goes the more likely they'll receive it. So I remember as a child trying to figure out how to make the ash go really high. And I figured it out! First you burn the edges and once they're burning you light the center. This way it burns evenly and stays in one piece and goes really high. So you can communicate; and I can talk to my grandpa, my grandma. Since learning Thay's tradition and practice, all these memories have come back to me, and memories of my grandpa and my grandma. Now I know that we can communicate with our ancestors.

That little room is where I sat when I was first learning meditation. I was in high school when I started to sit at the altar. I learned to sit with a stick of incense. The first time I did this, I burned a long stick of incense and said I'd sit until it finished burning. I couldn't do it, so the next time I broke off a shorter piece. I watched the incense burn; it was wonderful. If you have a chance to be in a nice quiet place to sit and watch incense burn, you can discover many, many wonderful things. I saw that when the ash falls off, the glow gets brighter. It was as if the incense was smiling at me. Sitting in a dark room, you can see the incense get dull, and then the ash falls and the incense glows again and smiles. This was how I learned to meditate. It's a wonderful way to start. The incense is a "friend" that helps you to focus.

Through my sitting, I began to see and understand more about myself. I saw that I had a tendency to get angry easily. Early every morning, my grandma would clean the kitchen and make a lot of noise while I was sitting. I would be so irritated. "Grandma, don't you know I'm sitting? It's so early in the morning, why are you cleaning the kitchen?" I could see my mind thinking like that and myself getting very angry. I'd try to wake up earlier to sit before she started cleaning, but I couldn't. But I'd developed this relationship with the incense. And while I was annoyed, the incense continued to smile at me. This was a gift. And I realized, "At least she's cleaning the kitchen." I saw she was just trying to help out my mom, so she wouldn't have to do it. I wondered, "What am I getting so angry about?" I sat and I began to see how my mind worked, that I started to get upset at things when I didn't understand them. So then when I heard my grandma cleaning, I'd smile, because I knew she was doing that to help out my mom. With that thought, the noise started not to bother me anymore.

I began to have a better quality of sitting and a better relationship with myself. I began to understand that my mind can be changed depending on how I look at things. Once in a while my father would wake up early, just after I'd begin my sitting. He'd come into the kitchen and start yelling at my grandma because he wasn't so happy with the noise either. My mind would turn to my father and be angry at him; and again, I'd see how my mind worked. Thanks to the medi-

tation and the incense that never stopped smiling at me, I realized, "Wow, this is all in my head." I'd want to get up and say something to my father right away, but because I'd promised myself to sit for the length of the incense, I really stuck to that. That's when I began to learn about dealing with my anger and irritation, and that it all starts in the head.

The Buddha said that anger is one of the three most powerful energies. Anger is a very powerful energy and it wants to come out. We do and say things that we sometimes regret. Anger is inside of us, but it can pop out because of something we see or hear. Right now we're not angry. But if someone were to say something unkind, or to take away something we were holding, we'd get angry. So our anger, we call it a seed, it easily pops open. If someone touches us or pushes us a little bit, we can easily be angered. We can become angry, but we can also know how to stop. That's one thing I learned sitting with the incense, that I don't have to do anything; if I'm angry, I can follow my breath.

Let's remember this next time when something makes us angry. If we're not sitting with incense, we can always put our hand on our belly and feel it expand and contract as we breathe in and out. Or we can go to our room. Or if there's nowhere else to go, we can go to the bathroom, put down the lid on the toilet and just sit there on the toilet and follow our breath, and say, "Anger is in me, irritation is in me, but I don't need to do anything until I'm calm. Otherwise, I'll say or do something I'll regret later."

When I was a child, I didn't have any tools like this. When I was angry, I ran away. One time I ran into the closet and I buried myself at the bottom of the closet, underneath everything, and I pretended like I ran away. I was really hurt, but I didn't have any way to handle it. But now, I can sit, breathe. And when we feel calm enough, we can go outside and say to our sister or our mother, "I just got very angry and I need your help." That's one thing we can try, belly breathing.

We can take ourselves away from the situation first. If our brother or sister is bothering us, we can remove ourselves from there. Go to our room. We can say, "I need to take a break, because I'm going to get very angry." This is one thing I wish all young people would learn, how to handle their feelings. Sometimes when we're feeling sad, we can do that. We can take care of it. Go sit and belly breathe. In, out. In, out.

Another gift I'd like to share with you involves our two hands. We can do this when our mom and dad come home. With our joined palms we make a flower that's blooming. So when we greet our mom or dad, maybe they came home from work and they're not so fresh, they're under a lot of pressure so they're not at their best, we can offer them a flower. Our mom is like a flower and our dad is like a flower, and we are like a flower bringing freshness to them. Our mom and dad need to be cared for too. What happens when we don't water a flower? It wilts. That happens to humans, too, if we don't care for each other, and if we're not loving to each other. Sometimes by the way someone looks or talks, we know that the flower needs to be watered. Those are the signs. When we see that, we join our palms as if to say, "Mom, here's a flower for you." It's like the bell; we can use it to bring mindfulness into our home and when we see our parents need our help. If our family has two or three kids, our mom and dad have to sacrifice a lot for us. And so sometimes they need us to understand them more and help them out. Sometimes if our mother has many things to take care of, she feels she's at her limit. Sometimes our father is at his limit. They do everything for us. They clean our clothes, they bathe us, they make sure everything we need is there—we don't know that when we're a child. They would sacrifice everything for us.

You know, parents are just big children. Maybe they grew up in a family that wasn't as loving as the family we're in now. Maybe our grandparents weren't nice to our mom and dad. But now they want to be different with us. They're like flowers. Once in a while we can write them a note, a card, and surprise them. So it's not always that the parents take care of us. We can take care of our parents. There are wonderful times. But there are times that they need our help, when they're at their limit. We make flowers in our heart, and we offer them a flower. "Daddy, here's a flower for you," and we smile. That flower is always there. So you don't have to run to the market to buy a flower. It's right there in our hand. We can all look at each other as flowers, no matter what age we are.

S H A R I N G S

Brother Phap Dong

It is the third day of the retreat. Arriving at the small cabin that has become the meeting place of sixteen "Sneezing Pandas," I see that a few young people have already arrived for this afternoon's children's program session. I join them, and we sit on the steps outside the front door chatting comfortably together, watching the adults go to their Dharma sharing groups beneath the spectacular backdrop of Rocky Mountain peaks. The air is becoming a bit cooler and we can feel an afternoon storm approaching. They ask me what my favorite flavor of bubble gum is. I tell them that it has been over four years since I last had a piece. Scandalized and amused they offer me a piece. I put in my pocket, promising to blow them a bubble when I try it later.

Suddenly, a flash of lightening streaks out above the mountains and the group grows silent. Seconds later, the thunderclap follows amidst their oohs and ahhs. The whole group has arrived by now and is sitting in front of the hut eyeing the mountain skies, eager to spot the next flash of lightning. We enjoy the show together simply and naturally, and there is a deep sense of friendship and connection among us—an openness and aimlessness that surprise me. I look over at Sister Blue Lotus. Our eyes meet and she silently transmits that she too is surprised by the depth and simplicity of this moment. Neither of us says anything. We turn back and continue to enjoy.

Moments like this contain the essence of the children's program. It is beyond pebble or snack meditation, beyond listening to the bell and feeling our bellies, though, indeed, it is rooted in activities like these. It is a simple being present with each other—children with children, children with monastics, and all with the moment—sharing in a heartfelt way. Thay has said that the way young people benefit most from a retreat is simply by being in the energy of the Sangha. These "pandas" have bathed in this energy and have been embraced by it. They have become it themselves. How else could these nine to twelve year olds with their iPods, cell phones, televisions, computers, and video games be able to let go of it all and sit with such wonder and satisfaction watching a thunderstorm? For them, it is a true return to youth—a return to that simple and pure place that is their very nature, yet which is so often obscured by fast-paced over-stimulation and consumerism.

So often I have sat and watched the young people look up at Thay during a Dharma talk with an open look of complete attention. Now they gaze at the mountains with that same look, and I know that Thay is continuing beautifully.

Thich Not Here by Phyllis Colletta

My sole motivation for signing up for a six-day retreat in the Rocky Mountains was to see Thich Nhat Hanh. I wanted to be in his presence, and for this I would put up with the vegan food, cramped dorms, and early wake-up calls. Like many, I'd read Thay's books and listened to his CDs, and I just wanted to absorb his peaceful energy. My friend Marty, upon hearing of my intention to sit in the mountains with the master for a week, enthusiastically insisted on accompanying me, even though she had no idea who Thich Nhat Hanh was and had never been on a retreat. In fact, she was a little wary of "all this Buddhist stuff," but I guess she needed a quiet vacation near some trees. So on Friday, August 21, 2009, we set off in Marty's convertible, headed for Rocky Mountain National Park, a more-than-middle-aged spiritual version of Thelma and Louise.

Thay's retreat was billed as a mindfulness retreat and the theme was "One Buddha Is Not Enough." We'd soon be grumbling that "One Thay Is Not Enough" either, but the registration process was hopeful, with some nine hundred folks mindfully not butting in line or getting cranky...yet. As we snaked our way from one card table to the next station for more information and instructions, I marveled at the mix: a grandmotherly woman from Wisconsin, a reluctant teenager, exhausted parents with kids, an old man in a wheelchair. Come one, come all to Thay's retreat. They were young, old, short and tall, and all looking for love in this, the right place. And all but Marty, I suppose, here to drink in Thay's wisdom. By 5:00 P.M. on a fine Colorado summer evening we were eating dinner in silence, and I was quietly excited about the 7:30 Dharma talk because I knew I would finally see Thay.

The YMCA campus hosting the retreat had been teeming with soundless movement, a brown wave of monks and nuns. We filed into the meditation hall that evening, being more reverent than usual just in case the teacher actually took notice. We sat quietly in chairs, meditated for ten minutes, listened to angelic chanting, and waited. The monastics gathered together on stage, maybe fifty of them, a strong hushed mountain of devotion. "I will now read a love letter from our dear teacher," one said. A letter? "'My dear friends,'" the monk began, and I'm paraphrasing here because the next line lost me completely, "'I write this letter from Massachusetts General Hospital.'" There was an audible gasp, and nine hundred people simultaneously gnashed their teeth.

Thay's letter went on to explain that he had a difficult lung infection that precluded him from being at the retreat. The doctors in Boston had insisted he stay in the hospital for fourteen days. He said that otherwise he was fine. But I sure wasn't. Within a microsecond of my mind comprehending the impossible—Thich Nhat Hanh not here!—the following flashed through my head, in no particular order: WHAT!!!???? He's not HERE? What the heck? What is going on? He's not coming to the RETREAT? And what are we supposed to DO? He's the only reason I came! NOW what? He's not HERE!? And so on. It doesn't take much to conjure up the vastness and intensity of complaint. Talk about your monkey mind. It was a jungle in there—in my head, that is.

Outwardly we sat like good little Buddhist students, pretending to remember that we should be concerned about Thay being sick but really just trying to stifle the guttural noises of disappointment. "So, he's not here?" Marty whispered innocently. I glared at her. It made no damn difference to her whether Thich Nhat Hanh was here or there. She didn't care. Good ol' beginner's mind. The evening ended with a monk reminding us about Noble Silence, that period of non-talking from the end of the evening activity until after lunch the next day. We filed out of the meditation hall, stunned. I'm guessing a few folks were sneaking on to their BlackBerrys to see about the next flight out. I continued to entertain the two year old in my head, until I got to my hot dorm room where my two aged roommates were grumbling their way under the sheets. We sort of glared at each other, sharing disgust at our bad fortune. Thay had never, ever, missed a retreat before. Figures.

Saturday morning I arose dutifully at 5:30 A.M. and pulled on warm clothes for the morning walking meditation. As always, a walk outside seems to clear up my mental garbage and today was a glorious Rocky Mountain show-stopping revue. Several hundred retreatants slowly came together into a coherent group of followers, walking silently in the dark behind a tiny nun. There's a morning twilight in the mountains that spills about five shades of white and gold over the peaks before the sun even pokes up, and there they were: splendid soft colors framing the skyline while the stars still shone bright. I breathed in deeply the chilly mountain air. It felt good to have these people walking slowly with me. Right by my side was a black man with the arms of a football player. In front was a young woman with a rose tattoo peeking out from under her shirt. In a split second the sun shone its first small beams over the mountains and immediately the coyotes began to yip and howl. It was amazing. I put one foot in front of the other.

From the other side of the park, another huge mass of quiet humanity moved together, slowly, across the dewy grass. Somehow we all met in the middle, nearly a thousand of us, sleepy but mindful. We sat down right there and breathed, surrounded by the Rocky Mountains, washed in cold clean air. It felt good to be free of my own incessant babbling about how disappointed I was. I just sat still with all these strangers, and felt better. We walked peacefully to the meditation hall, and sat again. Something began to shift softly inside me with the retreat routine in place. I felt safe, even held, with all these good folks on the path. Even though much of the day was spent in silence, we smiled deeply at each other as we passed on the sidewalk or sat across the table in the dining hall. We bowed every time another person came to eat with us, respectfully acknowledging a new presence.

It's a tradition on Thay's retreats to have a Buddhist Be-in on the last night of the gathering. We were scheduled to leave on Wednesday, so during Monday's small group Dharma discussion session we were told that as a group we'd have to come up with a creative "thing" to present at the Be-in. My mind resounded like a gong. I would write a poem and call it "Thich Nhat Here!" I couldn't concentrate for the remainder of the session so quickly were rhyming words flooding into my head. We left for dinner and Marty had no idea what was happening. "I need paper!" I said with a hint of desperation as we hoofed it to the dining hall. "Paper?" "Marty, I've got a poem coming in. You have any paper?" She rummaged through her backpack and handed me a notebook, still confused about what was "coming in" so quickly.

We ate in silence and it took all my discipline not to scribble things down while I focused mindfully on chewing each bite thirty times. There were colorful jingles dancing in my frontal lobe, like the Starbellied Sneetches. Indeed, more present to me than Thay right then, as I munched my tofu, was my hero Dr. Seuss. We sat outside in the cool evening after dinner, and Marty took out her knitting and started talking. "Hey, Marty, you gotta be quiet hon," I scolded, "I have to get this down." She crooked her head and squinted, shrugged, kept knitting. I continued to take dictation from Dr. Seuss. This is the creative process; I'd been through it before. You just act as a channel and it comes through you like a baby. But it can be frustrating when words get stuck and some things don't quite fit.

Rather obsessively, I thought about my Dr. Seuss poem for the next twenty-four hours. At Dharma discussion on Tuesday I asked my friends whether they might want to use my poem as our presentation. I read it, and they laughed and hooted. A musician in the group offered to put one of Thay's poems to music after I read my little bit. Just like that, we had an act. One of the women in my discussion group insisted that I put my hair in a ponytail on top of my head, "like Betty Lou Who." It's just amazing how Dr. Seuss brings out the best in all of us. I complied, of course, proud to be a Who, and we prepared mime and dancing to go with the poetry. It was fun, almost joyful, and no one had really talked about Thay's absence in days. We were absorbed in our community, our process, and that was that.

Tuesday evening we gathered in the hall for the Be-in and there was singing, dancing, and lots of laughter. After each act—some rather loud and raucous—a monk would invite the bell three times so we would all settle back down. When it came time for our group to present, my buddies were rubbing my head and wishing me well. It had hardly occurred to me that I'd be reading a Dr. Seuss poem to a thousand people while staring into a camera, recording the whole thing for Thay, with my hair in a ponytail on top of my head. Hmm. I stepped up to the microphone. "A poem in the tradition of the American Zen master, Dr. Seuss," I said. Some laughter. "It's called, 'Thich Nhat Here.'" The place exploded in guffaws. They laughed and laughed and I shrugged, letting the sheer happiness wash over us all for a minute. What had caused such suffering on Friday was now bringing the house down on Tuesday. Talk about transformation. Go figure. I began to recite the poem.

I wanted to sit at the feet of the master
When Friday I heard these words of disaster:
"I write this letter from Mass General," you said
And from 900 people, an audible dread.
I came to experience life without fear
And what do you know?
Thich Nhat here!

We came from Virginia, Montana, D.C.,
From the mountains and deserts, by land and by sea.
Spent money, took time, from far and from near.
And what had we heard?
Thich Nhat here!

Your brave monks and nuns did not miss a beat.
We sat there stunned, nailed to the seat.
A very good thing we had silence while dining;
In our heads, dear Thay, trust me we were whining.
My roommate was snoring, the room hot as hell
But your monks they were smiling and ringing the bell
And all we could do was to sit, sit, sit, sit.
And we did not like it, not one little bit.

But as the days passed, though we thought of
    you often
Maybe you did us a favor in Boston.
What we did learn with you far back east

Is we are the Sangha, we are the feast.
And who can contain your spirit so vast
In a body that's old and not built to last?

By Sunday I looked at my roommate so dear
And what do you know? Thay, he is here!
The doctors in Boston would feel much chagrin
To know you're here where the air is so thin.
You're here, dear teacher, as we walk in the dark
And sit in the hall and stand in the park.
Your monks and nuns, they did not miss a beat

They breathed and they breathed and they sat on
    their seat
And it dawned on us all as we sat very still
That you are the teaching as old as these hills
And we live the practice, we light the way
And wherever you go, Thay, and whether you stay
I look in the eyes of my roommate so dear
And what do you know,
Thay you are here!

There was not a sound in the meditation hall. I bowed to
them, my Sangha, and to the camera, for Thay our teacher.
Our friend played the guitar and sang one of Thay's poems.
I'm sure Thich Nhat Hanh could not have been more present if he was smack in the middle of the room. When I
walked off the stage, one of Thay's nuns asked me for a copy
of the poem, to give to Thay. Happily I handed it over. What
do you know? I'm having personal contact with the master
through a Dr. Seuss poem. Life is strange, no?

On our final morning together, many of us took transmission of the Five Mindfulness Trainings. We wore our best and sat together in the center of the hall. Those farther down the path sat all around us, surrounding us with love and support. The monks and nuns wore yellow over the brown. They were resplendent. During part of the ceremony we "touched the earth" and did prostrations to connect deeply with the earth's energy. Bowing deeply had never felt so good. As I put my forehead to the rug, I felt a wash of familiarity, like I had come home. When I first did prostrations years ago on a retreat I felt strange and awkward—who am I bowing to? I had wondered. No one, and everyone now was the answer. I could have spent the whole day on the floor.

a story
of
collective
awakening

5: A Story of Collective Awakening

Brother Phap Thanh

IN BUDDHISM we talk about "consciousnesses" in the plural. Think of a circle cut across in two parts. The upper part we call "mind consciousness" and the lower part we call "store consciousness." In our store consciousness there are numerous seeds of many varieties lying dormant there. One could be a seed of joy. Another could be a seed of anger. Another one could be a seed of happiness or sadness, and so on. From time to time, when a seed is triggered, it will come up and manifest in our mind consciousness. Once it manifests there, we call it a mental formation. When a seed is in store consciousness, it's dormant, so it's not there for us at that moment. When a seed becomes part of our mind consciousness, it plays a role in our life; it's an energy that is with us. Say the seed of joy was dormant and then it was triggered and it comes up into our mind. We may not yet be aware of it, but it is playing a part in our life at that moment. The same is true for the seed of anger or any other seed; when it's triggered it manifests in our mind consciousness.

Among the seeds in our store consciousness is a very powerful tool. It's a seed we call the seed of mindfulness. When we invite the seed of mindfulness to come up into our mind consciousness, it has the power to become aware of the other mental formations that are manifesting in that present moment. So when we invite the seed of mindfulness to come up, it can become aware of the seed of anger and embrace it. From that point on, we have a choice about what

79

we're going to do with that anger. Before the anger was manifesting, it was a seed in store consciousness, and we were mostly not aware of it. Store consciousness is the basis, the foundation. Mind consciousness can have a lot of power when we're able to use our energy of mindfulness.

The Four Right Efforts

There are four different ways we can practice with our mind. They're called the Four Right Efforts. The first Right Effort is a way of practicing with the positive seeds. There are a number of positive seeds in our store consciousness. They might be seeds of happiness, mindfulness, joy, compassion, loving kindness, equanimity. When one of those seeds manifests in our mind consciousness, we just try to keep it there as long as possible. This is the first Right Effort. Thay, our teacher, sometimes gives the example of looking at mind consciousness as your living room, and looking at store consciousness as your basement. You can invite a positive seed into your living room; it's like inviting a friend, perhaps the seed of happiness, to come into your living room. And you try to keep your friend as long as possible in the living room because that friend gives you pleasure, you enjoy being with that friend.

Yesterday morning, I felt the wonderful energy of mindfulness that had been generated by all of us together during the morning meditation. I noticed that my senses were much clearer, I was much more aware of the blue sky, the birdsong sounded more beautiful. I noticed that the seed of mindfulness had grown stronger and was present in me. I decided to not go directly to breakfast as I'd originally intended, but to just stay outside with that seed and enjoy it a little more. So I just sat down on the side of the road and enjoyed the sunshine. The sun was coming up, and I enjoyed the morning sunshine and then went for a little walking meditation to keep that seed in my mind consciousness a little longer. Then I went slowly to breakfast, still trying to keep that seed as long as possible. But we

have to also be aware that all the seeds that manifest in our mind consciousness as mental formations will also go away. They come and they go. It's wonderful to invite them to be in mind consciousness as long as possible. But we also need to be aware that at some point they'll go back to store consciousness. That's an especially wonderful thing when you look at your not so positive seeds and know that they all have the chance to go back to store consciousness and go back to sleep.

The second Right Effort is to invite the positive seeds in store consciousness up into our living room. In the basement, there are many seeds that have not yet manifested. You can help them to manifest in your mind consciousness by inviting them up to your living room to live with you. One way to do this is to train yourself to have those seeds come up a little bit more often. For example, you can do mindfulness meditation once a day in your daily life; you can try to include the energy of mindfulness in more of your daily activities; you can try to spend more time with people you really enjoy; you can have more moments of joy, more joyful activities. Try to find little pockets in your life when you can invite those positive seeds into mind consciousness. You can also practice, for example, to water the seeds of compassion and loving kindness toward other people. For example, some people do a good deed every day and help another person. Research has been done which shows that doing this brings a lot of happiness to the person doing the good deed, not only to the person receiving it. This is a wonderful way of watering a good seed in yourself and at the same time in someone else.

These are the two Right Efforts that are concerned with the positive seeds, but you can do something with the negative seeds too. The third Right Effort is when a negative seed has not yet manifested, and it is still dormant down there in the basement of store consciousness. The easiest thing to do is not to invite it to come up to your living room. You might have noticed that sometimes there are things that trigger the negative emotion in you. I know there are certain things that can trigger my anger very easily, or that can make me easily sad. The practice of mindfulness helps me to be aware of what seeds I have, what seeds are manifesting, and what kind of mental formations they are.

The practice of mindfulness is the basis that we need for all these practices. If we have a negative seed that's still in the basement, in store consciousness, we allow it to be dormant down there and try not to trigger it. The longer it remains dormant, the more difficult it will be for it to manifest later. The reverse is true as well. The more often we make a seed manifest, the more easily it will manifest in the future also. Try to help those negative seeds in your store consciousness and allow them to stay asleep down there.

The fourth practice of Right Effort is when a negative seed has already manifested and is present in your living room. You need to find a way to take care of it, to help it go back into store consciousness and go back to sleep. I'll share a few ways to do that. The basis of all of this is the practice of mindfulness. If a seed of sadness or a seed of anger has manifested in your mind consciousness, the first thing you need to do is become fully aware that this is a seed of anger; you need to recognize it. Without the practice of mindfulness, it's very difficult. The practice of mindfulness helps with that first step of recognizing a difficult seed in mind consciousness. I give the seed a name. If it's anger, I call it anger. I say, "Hello seed of anger!" If it's sadness, I call it sadness. Whatever it is, I give it that name. That is also the practice of mindfulness, to recognize what something is and call it by its true name.

In Buddhism, we say all things are impermanent. It's the same with mental formations. It happens to me quite a lot. A seed manifests, I observe it and I notice that at some point it changes. I just keep on following it and naming it. When the seed of anger changes into a seed of stronger anger, or less strong anger, maybe irritation, I give it that name, I keep following it in the present moment and recognize and name whatever it is right now. Recognizing it and naming it is the first and most important thing to do if you want to take care of your anger and any of the seeds that you want to help go back into the basement.

You have to pay attention to be sure that you don't judge yourself or judge any of your emotions. Any emotion, any seed that comes up is okay. That can be difficult sometimes, because we have a lot of ideas, perhaps from our childhood, that it's not okay to be angry. For some people it might be something else, maybe it's not okay to be sad. So we need to be very aware that we don't follow these judgments, that we just come back to simple recognition and know that everything that comes up is okay and just wants to be seen.

There's a calligraphy that Thay writes that I like very much; it's about accepting everything as it is in the present moment. The calligraphy is "This is it." It sounds very simple, but when you practice it, it's not as simple as it sounds. "This is it" basically means that whatever manifests at that point is simply recognized by us. It's okay that it's there and we don't need to change it in that moment. We just recognize it first.

The first thing we can do when we have a difficult emotion coming up is to embrace it with our mindfulness and to see how strong it is. Then we need to look at ourselves and ask, "Do I have enough strength right now to take care of it? Do I have the time and the energy right now to take care of that emotion?" We need to be very honest. If we say, "Right now I haven't slept enough, I'm very tired, and I haven't eaten well," maybe right now isn't a good time to take care of these emotions. What we can do at that point is to "change the CD."

You know sometimes when you listen to a CD, you'll notice this is not actually the CD that you want to listen right now, and you naturally go and change the CD. You can do something like this with difficult emotions when they come up. At the point you decide "I can't take care of it now," change the CD. Change it to a beautiful one, one that you know that you like. For example I like to go out for a walk in nature, I know that's a CD that I really like, and it's easy for me to change the CD when it means doing something that's very pleasant and wonderful for me. This is one thing you can do when you feel you can't properly take care right now of the difficult seed that has manifested. We invite positive seeds from our store consciousness into our mind consciousness to help, to gain more strength whenever we've noticed we don't have enough strength to take care of a difficult emotion, a difficult seed right now.

Something else we can do to gain more strength in everyday life in order to take care of the negative seeds when they come up is what I like to call "mental hygiene." Many of us have very good routines for taking care of our bodies, physical hygiene. For example, normally almost everyone here brushes their teeth at least once or twice a day; if you do it three times it's even better. There are other habits that we've acquired, like taking a shower regularly, washing our clothes.

All of these ways of taking care of our physical hygiene have become a habit. But not all of us have yet made it a habit to take care of our mental hygiene.

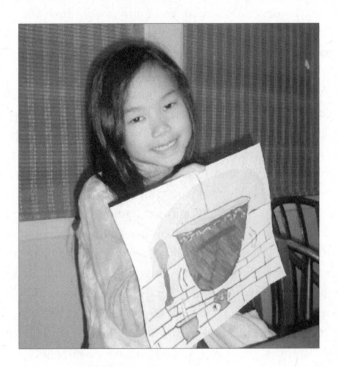

One of the things we can do every day is to sit down and practice sitting meditation, or to find time every day to practice walking meditation. Even if it's only walking from the car to the door of our house, or if it's only five or ten minutes in the morning for sitting meditation, that's already a very good start. This is something we do to nourish our strength. There are now some scientific terms for these things you can do to nourish your strength. There's something called the relaxation response. I've come across this recently and I like it very much. It's basically meditation, but it doesn't come from just one tradition of meditation. The relaxation response is the response that helps us to relax our body, to have more joy and peace. It's the opposite of the stress response. The stress response is well known to all of us. That's when we get very tense, and our heartbeat goes up, and we feel either the need to fight or flee. The relaxation response is the opposite. This was discovered when doctors and scientists studied meditators and saw in them the physical and mental opposite of the stress response. The relaxation response helps to calm you down and to activate the parts of the brain that actually make you steadier and healthier.

The relaxation response is something you can cultivate by, for example, doing sitting meditation. To elicit the response, you do something repetitive or you focus on one thing. For example, you repeat a word or you focus on your breathing. Or you can repeat a certain action, like doing walking meditation. The second thing you need to do is to always bring your mind back to that repetitive action. For example, in many spiritual traditions there are repetitive prayers. In sitting meditation we always come back to our breathing, and we bring our mind back to our breathing when the mind wanders off. In walking meditation we bring the mind back to the footsteps, to the walking. And when the mind wanders off, we don't judge it, we simply bring it back to the walking. And that brings about the relaxation response. It's as simple as that. This exists in almost all spiritual traditions. It's something we can cultivate in our daily life that will give us strength to take care of the more difficult seeds when they have manifested in our mind consciousness.

Another thing we can do when anger comes up is to embrace it. That is something I can do easily in sitting meditation. Some people do it in walking meditation. I basically bring up the image in my mind of my anger, what it looks like. For me this kind of visualization is very vivid. Mostly, my anger is a little boy or a little man who runs and jumps around, kicks everyone, and keeps going around in circles. That's usually how anger looks in my mind. You have to look in your own mind to see how your anger or other emotions look.

When I want to take care of my emotion, and I know I have the time and energy, what I do is to sit with it and visualize it and

embrace it. I see it and I embrace it. I can tell you for sure that sometimes it doesn't want to be embraced. I let it kick a little bit more,
and I'm just there for it with my presence. Then I try a little bit later
again, and later again. Because I know—this is what I've learned
from my teacher—that things are impermanent, so the anger will
inevitably change; and so far my anger has always changed! Sometimes it's just a matter of patience, being with it, and at some point
I'm able to embrace it. I have this image in my mind that I just take
it in my arms, this little anger, and then most the time it changes.
It's very interesting.

The next thing I do, once I've embraced it, is I take the time to
look into it, to look deeply at what's happening. And looking deeply
is essentially just sitting with it, observing it, and giving it space—
and also listening and watching what it's doing. Looking deeply is
something closely connected with insight or wisdom, which is very
different from knowledge or from knowing something about my
anger. I can do a lot research about my anger, but that mostly stays in
my head and doesn't really change anything in my whole being. So
I sit and look deeply into it. I just allow it to be there, give it space,
and try to be as open as possible, simply observing. I call it trying
to have a radical openness, because I need to be open so I can really
observe what's going on without any judgments.

When I have a judgment—for example from my parents or my
grandparents—that it's not okay to be angry, this already interferes
in the process and tells my anger to shut down and go away. So I
need to be aware of this part of my mind, too, and know that I have
these judgments. With mindfulness practice, I can just be present
and observe without reacting to it or judging it. This is looking
deeply—observing and being radically open. At that point I more
easily become aware of the impermanence of my anger. I continue
to observe it and see what it's doing. During that process of embracing and observing my anger, I've noticed it sometimes changing
into a sadness. Once the anger calms down, sadness may come up
that underlies the anger. Sometimes it may be something else that

emerges. And it's different in every person. So it's up to you in your own practice to look at what your little anger is doing.

Once I've sat with it for awhile—and I do this as long as I can, maintaining the energy of mindfulness—at some point I'll get tired and then I'll go and do something else. I don't force it. I'm aware that it's a process and can take a long time. Some of my habit energies have been with me for a long time already. Maybe some seeds were planted when I was very young, some of them very powerfully planted and watered. I know there are certain situations in which I react very strongly and anger comes up easily. I know these seeds are deeply rooted somewhere in my consciousness, and I need to take care of them over and over again.

However, every time I take care of such a seed—bringing up the energy of mindfulness, recognizing it, embracing it, looking deeply into it—it becomes a little bit weaker and usually I have learned a little bit more about it. It becomes a bit more of a friend than an enemy. This is very helpful, because each time I do this, it gives me a little more freedom not to react in a certain way and to see that I actually have a choice. I notice, when my difficult emotions are concerned, I can just react and go down the path of anger, maybe have a very angry conversation with someone. Or I can stop and maybe wait a little bit until the anger has calmed down, knowing that it has to do with my suffering from the past. Then later on, I can talk to the person that has triggered that anger and explain the situation. It's a very powerful approach when you practice mindfulness. It's something that can give you many choices.

Most of our negative emotions actually play out very unconsciously. They just follow their patterns, and some time later on we'll notice that we've just caused damage in our family by shouting at someone. Something just came up and played out without our being aware of it, without our mindfulness. But if you keep practicing with it, you'll have more awareness and more choice.

When we're calmer and have learned more about ourselves, we can act from a place of compassion and understanding toward other people. If I react directly from anger, mostly it's not very compassionate or understanding of the situation of the other person. Giving my anger or my sadness time to calm down, also helps a lot with the communication I have with other people.

When I sit and look into my emotions, it also helps that I remember I'm not this emotion only. Sometimes when a strong emotion comes up, I'm completely just this emotion. I'm only very angry, and I act out of that anger; it just seems to take over. But when I sit and just recognize it, embrace it, and look deeply, I notice that I'm actually much more than that emotion. Even in that moment when it's so strong, I'm much bigger than that emotion. The more I practice with it, the less it fills up my whole being and the less it takes over.

Namo'valokiteshvaraya by Miriam Goldberg

The first few hours: A cluster of brown on stage, the monastics a small singing mountain, calling forth an opening, inviting love and understanding, singing solidity, commitment, and love to a vast expanse in front of them. Namo'valokiteshvaraya...a tenderness, so vulnerable as each brown tree reaches into its roots, brings the purest intention to be present and strong, nourishing one another, coalescing a swaying invitation to us all in waves coursing through the hall.

Namo'valokiteshvaraya...a love letter from Thay, gentle rain falling on mouths still shocked, surprised, concerned, gentle rain offering the sweet taste of interbeing if we dare let loose our disappointment and fall into the Dharma moment of now where we can feel the swelling strain of bewilderment push the limits of our hearts, stretch the tenuous reach of the Sangha body, which is breathing timeless compassion to catch us, receive us, hold us, cradle us all.

Namo'valokiteshvaraya...the beautiful orientation to practice: being present with our body, breath, heart, and mind, touching that inner presence which births mindfulness, melts distinctions, and opens us into interbeing. Calling, calling, calling us to be present, to be the Sangha body which is nourished by the mere intention to be here. Namo'valokiteshvaraya...early morning, as the first glow of dawn bows to the night sky and lifts our souls to the infinite deep space, we are filled with a rarified air in and around us. We sit, both lightened and grounded, as our cells adjust to the mountains, the luminosity, the Sangha body we are becoming. In the meditation hall, a tender voice takes our hand and walks us into our breath where we can consider letting go of everything, for just a moment, just this moment, just this ever present moment, lay down everything until it drops through the breath, and in the breath our hearts rest on gentle, endless wings, in and out.... When meditation ends, the presence of Thay is unmistakable. We are a Sangha body, a living, breathing expression of love, understanding, and presence, a Buddha being manifesting. We are not alone.

Namo'valokiteshvaraya...that first Dharma talk without Thay present in the physical body to rivet my attention on him, my awareness naturally opens into the room. A subtle vibration is moving through the Dharma hall during the talk, very soft, very gentle. It is the feel of love. It is coming from the monastics. They are as a hive of bees gently humming, sending tendrils of praise and support to each other. They are nourishing each other, pollinating each other, sharing with each other, and the sweet scent and hum is spreading through the hall. We are being blessed, pollinated, and honeyed. Flowers are blooming. Seeds are quickening. We are humming. A hive. Alive.

Namo'valokiteshvaraya...as the retreat continues, the Sangha body strengthens, deepens, carries, cares, develops a precious closeness woven with fine invisible threads of love and appreciation spun from practice and awareness of brother, sister, compadre on the path, closer than friend. The Sangha body becoming a Sangha family, spreading, opening, including, laughing—threads spanning the earth, reaching and holding beyond time and space, alive with quietly felt mindfulness, heart-fullness, willingness to be present to the always nothing that is something, and gratitude to each of us who transmits and receives the teacher and the teachings, threads extending and melting. Namo'valokiteshvaraya....

Peter Poulides

My mother, Helen Poulides, died a few weeks before the Colorado retreat. She was ninety-four, in good health and high spirits, and loved by all who knew her. I had many friends who claimed her either as their own sister or mother. She died peacefully in her sleep. We were not ready for her to go, but she was very worried about dying slowly and painfully, and this is exactly how she would have wanted it. So when I sat in the beautiful new meeting room with hundreds of others on the first night of the retreat and heard the letter from Thay explaining his absence, the only thought that I had was "Of course!" I was trying to get used to life without my mother. Even though we all knew that she couldn't live forever, the older she got, the harder it was to imagine a world without her. So when I found out that Thay would not be with us in the mountains this year, it felt okay. Just as I am now what has been passed on by my mother, so would we all be without Thay. Seeing his family come together so strongly and surely, giving such beautiful and open-hearted Dharma talks, and taking care of us with such grace and humor was a model for me and my birth family. Thank you for that gift.

Walking At Sunrise by Sue Kronenberger

I see a man
among the peace walkers.

From the side
he looks like you—
the shape of his head
the cut of his hair
the way he trims
his graying beard and moustache.

My heart smiles at the thought of you.
I bring you into clear focus—
feel your arm around my waist
hear your voice whisper to me,
"you'll be all right."

The morning light nudges its way over the mountains
and we walk on, nearly a thousand strong.
Slow steps in peace
slow steps for peace.

Many couples walk hand in hand
arm in arm.
The man and wife in their seventies
weathered, a little bent.
A dad and his sleepy daughter wrapped in a blanket.

The two young sisters,
small only in physical stature
their brown robes brushing the tops
of worn athletic shoes.
Hands clasped, delicate fingers intertwined.
They lead us without speaking.
They invite us to walk with them
on the irresistible path.

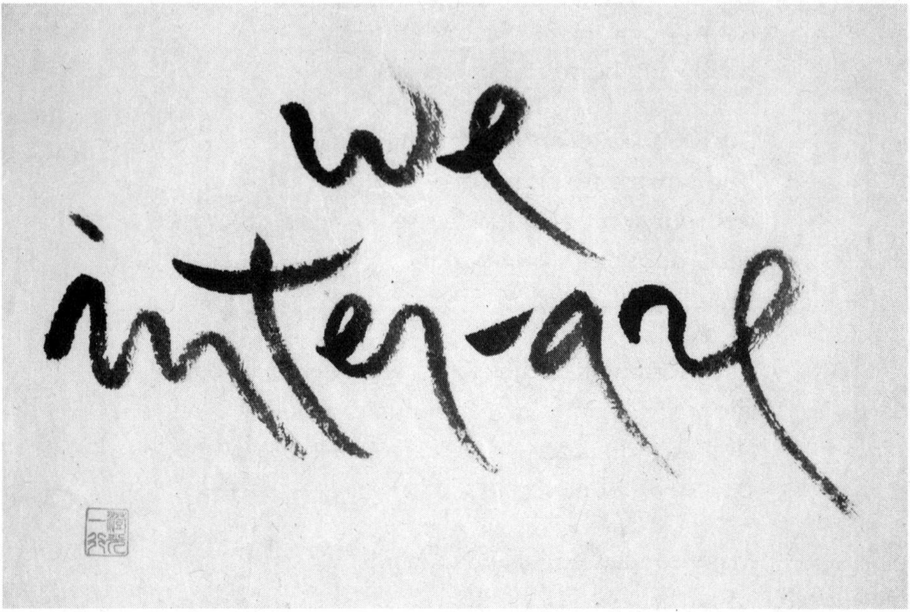
we
inter-are

6: We Inter-are

by Sister Dang Nghiem

ON THE FIRST day of the retreat, I said to myself, "These are the best moments of our life, aren't they?" I felt comfortable saying that, even though it was a challenging time for us as we adjusted to the situation that Thay couldn't come to the retreat. We monastics had to step up to lead the retreat, knowing that you have many aspirations and wishes when you come here. Yet, I was able to appreciate these best moments of our life. The brothers and sisters went hiking every day before the retreat started. I went swimming every morning. We drank tea, we sat, we talked, and we had several meetings.

I love the Dharma, because the Dharma teaches me and trains me how to live in the present moment, to rejoice with what is—the challenges, the difficulties, as well as the beauties and wonders in that moment. And the Dharma teaches me and trains me how to love. I have two beans that are quite special to me. A dear friend sent them to me last year on my birthday. When I became a nun, my friend was sad and confused. After I'd been ordained for a year or so, he came to visit me in Plum Village, and he said, "My mother asked when you will be coming home." It has been more than ten years now. I think he has come to accept my decision. And I have learned to love more deeply than I ever did before. This bean can illustrate that more than I can with my words.

The bean has the usual oblong shape, but then it has a line running right down the middle, dividing it into two halves. One half is entirely white, but it has a black dot; and the other half is entirely black, but it has a white dot. I think my friend ordered it online. They call them "Yin Yang beans," but he named them "inter-beans." All of us are "inter-beans." Maybe the word "interbeing" sounds theoretical or mystical. I think these "inter-beans" speak most clearly: In this, there is that. In the white there is the black, and in the black there is the white. This is in that, and that is in this. This is what interbeing means. It's a concentration, a topic of constant meditation. If we think, "I'm very special, I'm unique, I'm better than you," then in that moment, we're not inter-beans; we're just beans!

True Love

The teaching and practice of interbeing is the foundation of true love. According to the Buddha, true love is composed of four elements, which we call "the four immeasurable minds." The first immeasurable mind is loving kindness. The second immeasurable mind is compassion. The third is joy. The fourth is equanimity, which can also be translated as inclusiveness or nondiscrimination.

The first immeasurable mind is loving kindness. We may understand loving kindness as: "I vow to bring joy to a person in the morning." How do we bring joy to someone? Children bring joy very naturally by their way of being. As adults, in our own ways of being, we also bring a lot of joy to others. Loving kindness is also a practice of coming back to oneself. It's not about looking outside, asking whether I'm bringing joy or happiness to somebody. It's a practice of coming back and asking, "Am I able to bring joy and happiness to myself?" This is the spirit of interbeing. If I have joy and happiness in myself, then I have something to offer. If I don't have it in myself, then what do I have to offer? Peace activists want to bring peace to the world, but we know that many peace activists aren't always very peaceful. As monks and nuns, we have very ambitious aspirations: we want to bring liberation to all beings. Of course, in our daily life, if we're honest, we'll recognize that very often we're not liberated; we fail to touch joy in ourselves. What prevents us from being joyful? I believe the main factor is the sense of separateness, of alienation, of disconnectedness that we often feel and perceive. We're unable to touch and cultivate the interbeing nature in all life-forms in every moment.

Dr. Daniel Siegel wrote a book called *The Mindful Brain*. He and other neuroscientists and psychiatrists looked at the brain area immediately before the frontal lobe, an area called the prefrontal cortex. The prefrontal cortex is very developed in human beings. The cortex is like the bark of a tree; it has six layers. We consume sensory stimuli through our five sense organs: eyes (forms), ears (sounds), nose (smells), mouth (tastes), and skin (tactile objects). A sensory stimulus travels to the brain, through the mid-brain, and then through the layers of the prefrontal cortex. While the sensory stimulus is traveling upward from the sixth to third layer, the prefrontal cortex sends a message downward from the first layer toward the third layer, saying, "I know what this is. It is my child. It is a tree, a pond, a frog." The ascending information merges with the descending information and, already at this level, perceptions are made. The brain stops processing the sensory information further. This top-down influence habituates us, and we perceive everything through the filter of the past. Our child, husband, wife, a flower, and life become categorical, monotonous, and stale. We are unable to interact and connect with the person or the situation as it is in the present moment.

When we perceive a beautiful or pleasing object, it stimulates the emotion center to release hormones that bring about a feeling of pleasure or safety in us. But if the perception is of danger or discomfort, then we experience a "fight or flight" response, and adrenaline is released into the bloodstream, causing the whole body to react. This was a very important evolutionary development, because our ancestors—plants, animals, and humans—lived in the wild, and the capacity to process information quickly and to recognize danger immediately enabled them to survive. We have inherited that instinctual survival capacity.

However, through evolution, we have also developed a higher capacity of self-awareness, and of recognizing everything for its suchness—as it is. The Buddha is referred to as "the one who comes from suchness." If someone is a Buddha, then it means that this person is able to see and perceive others and the world as they are—not in terms of the past or as a category. The child of this moment is not the child whom we saw yesterday or in the last moment. If we have immediate perceptions and conclusions, then we don't see or touch the child. Similarly, when we've been in a relationship for a while, that person is just a person, and there's nothing more to it than that. We have enough stored information about the person. We look, but we don't see each other anymore, because our brain has shut down and shut him out. This can insidiously result in a sense of separateness, of isolation, of schism. This is something we have in each one of us, and I see that it's an obstacle to our happiness and joy. Habitual energy causes us to see our beloved as a category, but mindfulness enables us to see that person anew. Mindfulness enables us to touch life in all of its wonders and intricate connections.

This morning my monastic sister said to one of our brothers who led the walk: "Let's take another path because maybe people will get bored." It's only the third walking meditation, and we can already feel bored with the route! You see! As soon as we take a step in that direction, the brain sends down the message, "I have been there! I have done it!" Awareness enables us to not conclude so quickly and shut out our own life so quickly. Life happens in every moment, and awareness heightens our capacity to receive and to be happy with what is. When we have a path, it fosters our capacity to be happy. For example, in a relationship, we come together and make a commitment, because we see that there is a beautiful path and we want to share it together. As monks and nuns, we also make the aspiration to follow the spiritual path, not only for this life, but life after life. Yet, it's not easy. Just because we make a vow or a commitment doesn't mean we'll be able to live it. We have a built-in program that can prevent us from seeing the path new and fresh. The daily practice of mindfulness, as individuals and as a community, enables us to transform this tendency. In this retreat, I've had the experience of walking next to a stranger or a new friend and we look at each other, we smile. Even if we have never met each other before, our eyes are so bright, and our smiles so sweet and open. In this moment, we have a shared path. There is mindfulness in us, there is peace in us, and we are able to see one another. This is an intention and an energy that we need to cultivate again and again.

Breathing with Thay

In 2005, Thay returned to Vietnam for the first time after he had been in exile for almost forty years. In 2007, we went back to Vietnam with Thay for the second time. At the end of the first visit to

Vietnam, we established Bat Nha Monastery (Bat Nha is *prajña*, wisdom). At the beginning of the second visit, we stayed there. After we'd been there for a few days, I was asked to come see Thay. Thay said, "My child, Thay has been coughing a lot, and the sputum is very fishy!" I had a stethoscope with me, but I put it aside. Respectfully and carefully, I placed my hands on Thay's back. I asked Thay, "Would you please breathe just a little bit deeper than usual?" My hands moved slowly down along Thay's spine, from the upper lobes toward the lower lobes of the lungs. What was incredible was that the bones in my hands could feel Thay's breaths very clearly. The resonance and vibration of Thay's breaths was right in my hands. After only a few breaths, my breath also synchronized with Thay's breath, just like that, and I continued with my hands going slowly, slowly, slowly down along the spine and then down again a little further out to the sides. When we perform a physical examination on a patient, we can use our fingers as percussion on the lungs. If the lungs are healthy, then the percussion sounds airy and hollow. However, in the presence of an infection, the consolidation, the fluid-filled area, sounds solid. The air moved through Thay's lungs so strongly and the resonance of Thay's breaths was so profound that I can still feel them in my hands. At night when I'm not able to sleep or when my body is in pain, I place my hands—one on my heart and one on my abdomen and I just breathe. I breathe along with that breathing energy in my hands.

Soon after that, Thay was diagnosed with a pseudomonas infection in his lungs. It's usually an opportunistic infection that takes place in a hospital setting or when someone's immune system is severely compromised. Once the bacteria have a chance to proliferate, the patient often has to be on a respirator. Thay said to me, "Don't worry, my child, I will breathe them all out!" Since the beginning of 2007 until now, Thay has breathed them out and kept them under control! It is the power of mindful breathing! It is the miracle of mindful breathing! It has enabled Thay to continue to cultivate joy in himself. As Thay shared with us in his love letter from the hospital,

"It is only an infection." He has been able to be there to watch his monastic and lay students deepen their practice and grow. This is loving kindness, being able to embrace whichever condition life may bring and make it a part of her practice. Many of us have learned about mindfulness of breathing, but sometimes we may think, "It's just breathing! Everyone breathes." And then it becomes something not so important, something repetitive. But when I was able to feel Thay's breathing in my ten fingers, it changed my perception, and it changed my experience with breathing. To know what Thay has been able to do for himself and for all of us, given his serious health condition, also inspires me to truly practice.

We are very attached to our bodies. Even the Buddha went through sickness, old age, and death. Thay is a Zen Master, but above all, he is a human being. He, too, will go through sickness, old age, and death. We may claim to have a spiritual life, but if we continue to hold on to attachments just like in the worldly life, then we suffer. This is not true love.

Although I live in California and my teacher lives in France, I have learned to see Thay in myself. When I have a mindful breath, I am aware that I am doing exactly what Thay is doing. When I take a mindful, gentle step on the earth, I am aware that Thay is doing exactly that. In that moment, our interbeing is perfect. It's complete. I don't have any kind of complex that Thay is near, or Thay is far; Thay pays attention to me, or Thay does not pay attention to me; Thay knows me, or he knows me not. Maybe you've never met Thay in person. However, if you touch the miracle of your own breaths—how they bring you peace, how they slow down your mind—and if you touch the miracle of your own steps—how they bring you back to the moment and how they enable you to enjoy something as simple as the yellow flower in the sidewalk—then you are with your teacher. If you have learned something and made it a part of your life, then the teacher becomes a part of you. The teacher becomes you.

Compassion is the second immeasurable mind of love. We define compassion as "helping another person to relieve suffering." I trust that all of us aspire to help others relieve their suffering. But what I find interesting is that we are very addicted to our own suffering! A few weeks ago at Deer Park Monastery in San Diego, a young woman came to visit and practice with us. She was very good looking and talented, but she looked extremely distraught. At one point, I looked into her eyes and said to her, "Your best romance is your suffering." She was stunned. I told her, "Yes, you are very attached to your suffering. Even though you say you don't want to suffer, if someone were to touch your suffering, you would defend it. You would become very offended, and you would be willing to push everybody aside, even your parents and your partner, in order to curl up with your suffering."

Many of us are addicted to our suffering, physiologically and mentally. I think of an emotion, whether it's positive or negative, as being like a wave. We often see our emotion only in its aftermath. We may shout, "I'm not angry; what are you talking about?" But afterward, when the body is still shaking, we may admit, "Maybe I

was angry." We see our emotions, our feelings very late. But a wave doesn't start at its peak. It starts way before that. Beneath the surface of the water, the wave has started miles back. And it has worked up its momentum until the moment it surfaces. In Vietnamese we have a saying that a practitioner is like a fragrance going against the wind, or water going against the current. As practitioners, slowly we learn to go backward on the wave. First, we need to have simple recognition: "This is anger" or "this feels like jealousy or competiveness or self-doubt or self-promoting." If we can recognize it, see it as it is, or even if we can only say, "there is an emotion here," already that is awareness, and already it's different from the many times we weren't able to recognize it. Slowly, we learn to recognize it when it's at its peak. It's like when a drunk person is able to say, "Yes, I am drunk," instead of "No, I'm not drunk." Mindful breathing helps us with this. The physiology of breathing is amazing. The body always wants to maintain a balance, homeostasis, a consistent level of oxygen concentration, CO_2 concentration, and so on. So when there is a perception of danger or of dislike, adrenaline and various hormones are released into our bloodstream, and it affects our breathing. When our breathing is faster, shallower, it's because it's trying to compensate and bring back the balance in the body, as well as to tell us something is going on, that there's physical or emotional stress. But because we're not aware of our own emotions and what's going on inside us, this way of breathing becomes our habitual way. Many people breathe only at the throat or chest level, and that means a state of constant stress. Pain and stress are the body's SOS. But if we don't take care of them, they become the norm, until one day we break down with a physical or a mental illness. And there's plenty of that in our society!

As civilized human beings we've created more stress for ourselves. Even the telephone can bring us stress. We hear the phone ring and immediately we tense up and hold our breath and reach for the phone or run to the phone. At the practice center we use the phone, the chime of the clock, and so on, as a chance to stop and breathe: in, out. With that practice of coming back to our breathing, we're cultivating Noble Silence of body and mind, not doing or saying anything. When we're quiet, we can hear our thoughts. If we never stop and recognize them, these thoughts accumulate. "She doesn't like me," and so on, and all of a sudden, we feel anger, insecurity, jealousy, simply because in the beginning, when it was only a thought, we didn't see it. As practitioners, we learn to trace the wave backward so that we see it much earlier. And the moment we see something and recognize it as it is, we see that we have a choice. We can go along with the momentum and get all worked up. Or we can break the wave very early, even when it's only an incomplete thought. But that takes practice. And that is compassion; that is helping to relieve suffering. Many of us are addicted to our suffering and it becomes a part of our physiology and our mental state. A stimulus immediately leads to a response, and the response is a destructive wave of emotion. If you have been abused or traumatized in your life, and if you continue to go through this wave again and again every time you see, hear, taste, smell, touch (or be touched by) something that reminds you of the past, then the whole cycle of stimulus-response repeats and reinforces itself via the neural pathways. A single thought or a dream about the past can also trigger this entire stress response. That is why time does not heal. We suffer more and more. We become more and more angry, and more and more unhappy, and not so compassionate to ourselves and to others. Suffering does not bring compassion. Suffering can make people quite bitter and ruthless. Suffering can make people say, "I have suffered; you don't know what suffering is." But the understanding of suffering and taking care of suffering helps us to break that cycle, helps us to understand another person's pain, and makes us never again want to cause pain to another person. It is a training, and it is a practice. This is understanding the nature of interbeing; my suffering is your suffering, and your understanding is my true love.

S H A R I N G S

Claudia Crawford

Doing walking meditation with the monks and nuns and other retreatants early in the morning, stopping to see the dawn breaking over the beautiful mountains, was incredible. As we walked, stopped, and walked again, it felt as if we were one body. The beauty of the walking monks and nuns brought tears to my eyes.

Eating very slowly, chewing each bite so thoroughly, put me into meditation. I found myself looking around the room at all of the people, observing what they were doing, and feeling as if I was in a dream of aware detachment. I so much appreciated the long periods of silence, especially at meals. I found that each day I took less and less food, even though my first day's portions were moderate. The bowing to each other during meals always brought the most beautiful smiles to people's faces. In silence as they ate or sat, faces were calm, stern, busy with eating. But during the bow, each face bloomed like the most beautiful lotus.

Although I've been reading volumes of Buddhist sutras, commentaries, stories about Zen masters, etc., I had never joined a Buddhist Sangha. But one of the very clear messages of the retreat was "Sangha." The retreat itself built a Sangha of almost a thousand people. There was no one, as far as I could tell, who didn't feel connected—indeed, interconnected—in the assembly hall, during meals, in other activities, and just walking around in the beautiful mountain setting. It was remarkable how the hundreds of people who had come to see Thich Nhat Hanh were soon able to overcome disappointment and not only participate fully in the retreat, but genuinely feel—through the deep teaching of interbeing—a true oneness.

The monks and nuns were gentle and sweet and what they shared was inspiring. They were full of joy, optimism, caring, and giving. It was wonderful to see how they related to each other, even though living together can be full of challenges; they said they have many sessions of Beginning Anew! Their beauty was that of those who have truly practiced, some for many years. I was immeasurably changed by those short five days. Yes, there is a baby Buddha in the heart of each of us. "A lotus for you, a Buddha to be!"

Smiling With Thay by Brian Kimmel

When I learned that Thay was in the hospital, my immediate response was sadness and grief. There were many tears that evening. I went to my room, but could not sleep. Something was stirring inside of me from a very deep place. "Where is Thay, anyway?" "Where is this person I call, 'Teacher'?" "Is Thay inside or outside of me?" I thought of the many times I took Thay's presence for granted, feeling a little tired sitting at his talks, or a little bored during our walking meditations together, and doubting the effectiveness of the practices he was presenting. But with my new realization of Thay's impermanence, a different picture appeared. I started to ask different questions. "How can I see Thay, know Thay, and continue walking and sitting with Thay for many years to come?" "What part of Thay will live on even after the body we see as Thay decays?" It is the part that is Thay's true nature. We have a saying that is chanted after offering incense, to open a practice called Touching the Earth. The saying goes like this: "The one who bows and the one who is bowed to are both by nature empty. Therefore, the communication between them is inexpressibly perfect."

In everything that I am doing, I can see the body of my ancestors—both blood and spiritual ancestors. I am a continuation of many people and things. Likewise, I continue in many people and things. I cannot really be separate from everyone and everything I love, because we are products of similar elements coming together to form a body and mind. Live knowing you are the embodiment of your ancestors. Live knowing future generations will continue you. We all have the capacity to live this way. No one really has to die. The task, then, Thay asks of us, is to smile.

Debbie Reid

Upon hearing of Thay's absence in Colorado, what came to my mind was the night when I was a teenager and learned that my brother had been shot and might not live. I'd cried and cried and couldn't sleep. I got up out of bed and walked into my brother's empty bedroom. As I stood in his room, I called out saying, "I don't know what to ask for! I want my brother to live; I want him to come home. And yet is that what's best for him? I don't want him to be away or to die. And yet I don't want him to suffer. I don't know what is best for him." And I looked upward through my tears with my hands open and cried out, "I don't know what to ask for!"

Suddenly all that was in my brother's room, all that appeared solid, including his solid wood furniture, became beautiful colored dots. And amidst this beauty there was so much love, as if I were swimming in love, that I and all that is are love. And with this, the knowing that whether my brother comes home or lives or dies, all that is love. Our true essence is love, there is no here or there, there is no death. And as Thay says, "We inter-are."

With this remembering I realized Thay is here and I am with Thay; we inter-are. I thought of the chant I had been singing on my drive up to the retreat: "No coming, no going. No after, no before. I hold you close to me, I release you to be so free, because I am in you and you are in me."

Watching the Moon With You
by Victoria Emerson

Dear Thay,

I am sitting outside the dining hall watching the full moon rise over the mountain. Perhaps you are looking at the moon from your hut, too. Physically, I do not see you at this exact moment. But if you are looking at the moon, and I am also, then we are connected by our experience of the moon.

I was in Estes Park for the One Buddha Is Not Enough retreat. Physically, I did not see you, yet I felt your presence very deeply. When we who were hoping to go through lay ordination with you at the retreat learned you would not physically be present with us, we made a vow to show you our respect by deepening our practice. We felt it was the best way to wish you a speedy recovery and also we wanted to demonstrate that lay practitioners, not just monastic disciples, can practice mindfulness, compassion, and understanding.

As we exited the meditation hall into the midnight-blue dome of a star-studded sky, I was awestruck by the ribbons of silent retreatants weaving their way in absolute stillness to accommodations situated north, south, east, and west.

There was no bumping—only a gentle slow ballet of mindful moving. It reminded me of that night in Ho Chi Minh City in 2007 when we walked in silence to the river with our paper lotus boats and candles—a sacred moment. This remarkable silence was maintained day after day for sixteen hours at a time. You were with us in that silence. It impacted us all.

Dear Thay, I want to close this letter by sharing what I recently told my mentor Chan Huyen: "I have truly dropped my worries. Nothing seems to bother me anymore. There is a wellspring of joy that has replaced my anger. I am at peace."

Megan Sarnecki

The Colorado retreat was my first real exposure to Buddhism and my first ever meditation retreat. I came to meditation ten years ago when I was in medical school. I very much took to the practice and ideas that it brought into my life, but Buddhist groups scared me a little because I was not Buddhist.

My experience at the retreat was transformative. My first Noble Silence, my first experience eating many meals mindfully—and in the presence of hundreds of others doing the same! I am so grateful for the experiences the nuns and monks provided us and am grateful to have found a community back home to strengthen my practice. And finally, I now find the Buddhist elements comforting instead of frightening.

Thank you for bringing us your traditions and your calm natures so that we could all learn from each other and ourselves in such a wonderful environment.

Julie Gordon

The 2009 Colorado retreat was my and my son's first retreat and I felt Thay's presence right away on the stage. It was much later that I found out he was not going to be attending (in body). There were a lot of upset people. But perhaps because I really had no expectations of what a retreat was supposed to be like, and because I felt he was really there through the monks and nuns and people who attended the retreat, I had nothing to complain about.

I went through what seemed like layers and layers of emotional energy. On the last day it was interesting to note that I was not so emotional anymore. I had gone into a deep, meditational space that felt a lot better.

The eating meditation was a bit difficult for me but I did learn that my eyes are bigger than my stomach. Too often, I took a little too much food although I couldn't tell when I was putting it on my plate. As a fast-paced eater, it took some doing to slow down and enjoy my food.

One thing that I took home with me is the walking meditation. I do try to walk and breathe and be aware of walking and breathing. I was thinking about the phrase "Remember to breathe and to smile," which my son and I first saw upon registration. It made us both laugh, especially when my son did it in an exaggerated way. I remember that whenever I am having difficulty with just breathing and smiling.

I turned fifty on the first day of the retreat. My mom was disappointed that I wasn't spending my birthday with her, and some friends thought I should have had a big party, but being in Estes Park was the best thing I could have done for myself and my son.

the
miracle
is to
walk
on Earth

7: The Miracle Is to Walk on Earth

by Sister Chau Nghiem

I'D LIKE to share with you a little bit about my happiness at the Stonehill retreat we just had last week. I had a chance to have my two nephews and niece with me then. My oldest nephew, Yared, is eleven; my second nephew, Yacob, is eight; and my niece, Galila, is six. I'd already taken my nephews to three retreats, so this was their fourth time. But it was my niece's first time, because she was just old enough to join the children's program. We had a wonderful time driving up together from Washington, D.C. to Easton, Massachusetts, where Stonehill College is. We had some adventures on the road, getting lost—we had poor directions—and so I asked the kids to help me to look out for the street we needed to find on the left. And Galila, my niece said, "Okay. Yared can read a little bit better than I can, but I'll try; which way is left?" I was so touched by her willingness to help! So I taught her how to tell your left hand from your right. When you hold up your left hand with your thumb out it makes the letter *L*, so you know that's your left hand. Now she knows which way is left.

Something I really enjoy when I'm with my niece and nephews is telling bedtime stories. We cuddle up in bed together and they love to hear stories about the Buddha. All the stories I know about the Buddha come from a wonderful book written by our teacher, Thay, *Old Path White Clouds.* I think it's my favorite book, and if you haven't read it, try to read it or ask your parents to read it to you.

I usually give them a choice of different kinds of stories I can tell: either about me and their dad when we were little, or true stories of animals helping people. But invariably they always want to hear stories about the Buddha. So I just share story after story until they fall asleep. One night, I was so tired that I fell asleep in the middle of the story, and they woke me up asking, "What happened next? What happened next?" I was saying something in my sleep, not at all related to the story!

What I enjoyed so much was the chance to have my blood and spiritual families come together, for the monastic brothers and sisters to meet my niece and nephews, and for them to meet my monastic brothers and sisters. They enjoyed playing in the children's program and eating yummy food. They really love choosing the kind of food they like and getting to go back in line at the cafeteria and having more autonomy over their food. They really like getting to know the other children, and sitting quietly, listening to the Dharma talk.

Thay said something at the retreat in Stonehill that really struck me. He said, "What children benefit from the most at a retreat is the Noble Silence." It's the collective energy of peace that the whole Sangha generates together. What children benefit from most is not words, it's not activities or games, but it's quietness and peace. And I think that—more than anything else—is what brings my niece and nephews back each time. Whenever I invite them to come to a retreat, they always want to come. When Yacob knew that there would be another retreat in October at Blue Cliff, he asked: "Can I go to that one, too?" During the Stonehill retreat, we'd call their mom and dad each night, and on the third day of the retreat Galila told her mom, "I want the retreat to be a week longer!"

So I think the quiet peace that we generate together is really what brings happiness and makes them content. It's possible to be happy without doing anything. You don't have to always have a game to play, or friends to talk to, or a place to go, or something to watch on the TV. In our daily life, we sometimes feel we must always be doing something, consuming something, taking something in with

our eyes or our ears. At a retreat we have the chance to find a deeper happiness that comes from really being there for each other. Our parents slow down; they're really there for us. And we can also really be there for our parents and our siblings. At a retreat, both adults and children learn how to be in a quiet place, to look at our fear about not doing anything—because we all have a fear, a discomfort that arises when we are not engaged in something. We think we could be doing something more fun, or be somewhere else, or with somebody else, or we just want something to occupy the time. So in a retreat, we find that we have a chance to take care of this energy of boredom and restlessness. We can find that just sitting quietly, listening to the bell, listening to our friends sharing, being with the monks and nuns is already a big happiness.

Our society also teaches us and pushes us to try to fill up the space, to always be reading something, watching something, doing something. So we need to create spaces that are safe for us just to rest, and to come back to something deeper inside us. Something I see in myself, and that I see in young people and in older people too, is that we run after pleasant things. If there's a good TV show we like to watch, we just want to watch it continuously. My nephews and niece have a DVD with many episodes of *The Simpsons*, and they want to watch one program after the other, without stopping. My brother told me that the kids "just melt into a pile of goo on the floor after a while." So we want whatever we like to continue, we don't want it to stop. I'm like that sometimes with a really good book. I don't want to stop reading even though it's time to go to bed and I'm tired. I want to keep reading because it's so interesting. Maybe some of us are like that with our favorite foods; we take more than we can actually eat because it tastes so good, but then we have a stomachache. Or maybe we have a friend that we really like; we want to be with that friend all the time, we don't want them to have other friends. We want that friend to only love us, to only be with us; maybe we get a little jealous when that friend spends time with someone else.

So we want to keep that sweetness and goodness, we want to hold on to it and we don't want to lose it. But we all need balance in our lives. Our friends are just like us; they need space to be happy and to grow. We need to give each other space, and give ourselves space. And when we don't eat too much of our favorite foods, or we don't watch our favorite programs all the time, we can appreciate them more. We need to learn to practice moderation.

When we come to a retreat, we learn to appreciate little things, and we learn to enjoy not doing so much. One time, early in the morning, just as the sun was coming up, I was doing walking meditation around the lotus pond of the New Hamlet in Plum Village. I was just walking by myself, really enjoying the quiet of the morning and the sounds of animals, the sounds of life around me beginning to wake up. And as I walked, really enjoying each step on the damp earth, suddenly from a few steps in front of me, I heard "plop!" Do you know what it was? A frog jumped into the pond, because he or she must have sensed that I was coming close. And that sound made me smile. And I smiled not just with my face, but with my whole body. I was so thrilled to hear the sound of the frog jumping into the pond; I felt that sound was a beautiful bell helping me to wake up. That sound is still nourishing me, even though it's already been five years since I heard it. I was able to enjoy that sound because there was space in my mind; my mind was quiet. If I'd been listening to music or talking to a friend or thinking about this or that, I wouldn't have heard that sound, and it wouldn't have touched me so deeply. I might have missed it completely! So the sound, the frog, the pond, the morning were all teachers coming to help me—to help me wake up and live my life deeply, and to feel how connected I am to all the things around me.

So, let's look at how we live in our daily life. What are the things that we're taking in, the things that tell us we have to keep taking things in until we don't have any more space inside, until we can't think for ourselves and make good decisions for ourselves. How can we create space so we can we let the world in? How can we not just live on the superficial surface of life, but really go deep and touch what is important, touch what will really nourish us and help us in our relationship with our parents and friends?

You may have touched this place when you do sports. Have you heard of "the zone"? Have any of you been in the zone before? Maybe when you're jogging or on the basketball court or hiking up a mountain and you begin to be really focused, really there with whatever you're doing. Maybe you've felt it when you listen to music or play music, or when you're writing or doing art, or talking and listening deeply to a friend.

At the retreat, when we learn about breathing and when we stop with the bell, that is to help us to find that zone in us where we can be really content with things just as they are—we don't need anything else to happen or for anything to change; we can be peaceful and at ease right where we are. Let's all reflect together on how to take the retreat home with us. The five days that we're together, we live very deeply. How can we continue to bring these gifts of the retreat back with us when we go home?

We can start every day with breathing mindfully. When we wake

up and we're lying in bed—as long as we don't fall back asleep!—
we can put our hands on our belly and we can breathe in and out
and know that we're breathing in and out. We can be aware of our
whole body, and relax our whole body. Or we may like to sit with
our parents, with our family, with our partner in the morning, and
start the day by touching this stillness and peace that are in each of
us. You can also take some time before you go to bed to lie down,
relax your whole body, and go through the events of the day—just
breathe and release the whole day, let it go, and allow your body to
really rest and sleep.

Those of us who live at the retreat center in Germany have been
invited to teach a class at the local public school. We teach a class
every week to children from twelve to fourteen years old, and we just
teach them what you're learning here at this retreat. We call the class
"Take it Easy and Be Yourself." The students love to do deep relaxation. At the end of our first term together, I asked them what they'd
learned that they were really using in their everyday life outside of
the class. Almost all of them said, "I do total relaxation before I go
to bed." One girl said she stands in front of the mirror and relaxes
each part of her body.

Learning to relax can help us a great deal with all aspects of our
life. A young boy who comes to Deer Park said that before he takes a
test at school, he closes his eyes, breathes in and out, and he relaxes.
He says now he does better on his tests because he knows how to
breathe. Many teachers bring a bell into the classroom, they bring
mindful breathing to the classroom, and their classes are doing better because of this practice of awareness, of being in touch with their
breath and their body. The children learn better and they have fewer
conflicts and difficulties with each other.

Before I came to this retreat, I was visiting my mom in Denver for
a few days. We went to the Denver Museum of Science and History
where there was an exhibit on the human body. At the exhibit there's
an activity in which you sit across a table from your partner. In the
middle of the table is a magnetic ball, and close to each of you is a

goal. Each of you puts on a headband with metal sensors that detect your brain waves. Next to the table is a screen that displays how relaxed or how active each player's brain waves are. The point of the game is to relax as much as possible and when you're fully relaxed, the ball will start to roll toward your opponent's goal. And if your opponent begins to be even more relaxed than you, the ball will start to roll back in your direction. I watched a grandma and granddaughter play this game. It was a real tight competition, the ball kept rolling back and forth and I saw both of them trying to relax more and more. The granddaughter relaxed and let her head drop forward, and then the grandmother, peeking at her, tried to out-relax her and let her head rest in her hands. Amazing game! I think we should all play this game. I think this is what life is like. The more relaxed we are, the more still and peaceful, the more we can accomplish, and the more effective we are. You may think that with all this meditating, stillness, and quietness, you can't be very effective in the world, in your job, or in school. But many people have brought mindfulness into their daily lives and have made a huge difference, not only in their own life, but in other people's lives as well. So to be mindful doesn't mean you can't be active or effective in helping other people, in healing suffering, and bringing joy to others.

A good example of this is Cheri Maples, a friend of mine. Until a few years ago she was a police captain. Cheri was a wonderful, wonderful police officer. In many places, police officers are known as "peace officers" and in her case it's really true. Maybe ten or fifteen years ago, she came to a mindfulness retreat and learned about the practice. Then she began bringing the practice to her police department, and she shared mindful breathing, mindful walking, and deep listening with her coworkers. In 2003, she helped to organize a retreat for police officers. Because of their practice of mindfulness, the level of stress and violence and suffering has gone down in the police officers and in the community.

Cheri is just one example of how we can bring mindfulness practice into our homes. We can have a bell in our homes and use it. Thay tells the story of a family that came to Plum Village and learned the practice. There were maybe four children in the family and they all learned about stopping and breathing with the bell. A few months after they went home, an argument erupted and everyone in the family was shouting at each other. They'd forgotten about mindful speech and deep listening. And the youngest child in the family, aged four, went over to the bell where it was on the altar, and she invited the bell. And everyone in the family stopped; they all remembered that they had been in Plum Village. They looked at her and they burst out laughing. So you children can help each other, and you can help your parents, you can help bring back peace and harmony in the family when there is tension or arguing.

Thay asks each family to set up a breathing room when they get home, to have a room that's just for coming back to ourselves and cultivating silence and peace in us. We have a dining room, we have a bedroom, we have a living room for guests, we may have a game room, a TV room, but we so desperately need a breathing room, a room where we can come and be really safe. In that room, when we go there to breathe and be calm, no one can come and pull us out. We don't answer the phone in that room, we don't watch TV in that room, we just breathe; we touch the Buddha in us in that room. Thay says: "When every home, every apartment has a breathing room, then that is civilization." When I was in college, my roommate and I had a closet and we used that as our breathing room. We had to take turns because it was too small for both of us, but we would breathe in there. So maybe when you go home, you can talk to your parents, to your partner, to your family about creating a space where you can breathe.

At the European Institute of Applied Buddhism where I live, I use our meditation hall. That is our breathing room, and it is also the place to resolve conflicts when I have difficulties with a sister. It's very helpful to have a place to go to talk. We both sit down on cushions on the floor. We have the altar there, we have the energy of practice in that room that helps us to let go, to forgive, to speak more lovingly, and to be more accepting of each other. So you may like to use your breathing room to do beginning anew and to resolve conflicts. If you don't have an extra room in your house or apartment, you can make the corner of one room into that special place.

Maybe you can think of ways to have a portable breathing room as you go throughout your day. When you go to the toilet, nobody can see you there or tease you for taking your time to breathe. When you're at school or at work, you can go to the toilet and you can stay there for just three in- and out-breaths. Just relax your whole body, and that is your private little breathing room. Or when you get a drink of water in the hallway of your school or where you work, you can breathe in and out and enjoy drinking the water. Think of that water fountain as a bell of mindfulness, and whenever you go to get a drink, you stop and really allow yourself to relax. When you have lunch, you may like to really look at the raisins, or the piece of apple, or the granola bar that you're putting in your mouth and really savor it, chew it, and enjoy it. You may want to eat a little bit slower than you usually do. And maybe your friends would like to join you, and you could have a dessert meditation at the end of your lunch; and you eat your pudding or your jello; you can have a contest to see who can eat the slowest, and you just enjoy every bite of your dessert, and smile to each other. Mmm! So yummy! And take your time. So that can be a part of your breathing room at school or at work.

I want to tell you a true story. In Pakistan, there was a young boy named Iqbal Masih. His family was very poor and when he was four years old, his family needed money so badly that they sold him into slavery. He had to work in a carpet factory. Because he was still very young, he had small fingers, and you need small fingers to be able to make the small knots at the end of the carpet. So he had to do that and work at a loom, weaving the carpets. He worked twelve hours a day, six days a week, from age four until about ten, with very little food, and no chance to go to school. Then when he was ten, he was able to escape and join a humanitarian organization that was trying to end child labor. He actually became an internationally known figure with this organization, going around speaking about the real suffering of child laborers. But some of the people in Pakistan who ran the carpet factories—they were called the carpet mafia—murdered Iqbal when he was twelve. There was a young boy, also twelve, in Toronto, Canada, named Craig Kielburger. He read about Iqbal's death in the paper, and his life changed when he read that article. He thought, "I have to do something." And he didn't know if he would get support from his friends. But when he shared Iqbal's story with his class, eighteen students were ready to volunteer to help him.

Together they started an organization called Free the Children. They researched as much as they could about child labor, they contacted other organizations, and a year later, Craig was invited to travel to Asia and visit children and listen to them share about what it was like to be a slave, having to work all day long under very difficult conditions. His parents didn't want him to go because he was only twelve; but he was determined to go. He sold his toys, the kids organized garage sales, and his parents saw he was really determined. Donations began to flow in as the group got more attention. And so he went on this trip; he went to Pakistan to visit where Iqbal was buried. He also went to Nepal, to Bangladesh, to Thailand, and he interviewed children there. In India, I believe, he asked for an audience with the Canadian prime minister who was visiting there at the time. And the Canadian prime minister didn't have time for a twelve-year-old boy so he ignored the request. But when the media began to report about Craig's work and the wonderful things his organization was doing, the prime minister took the time to meet with Craig.

After that visit, Craig and his organization of children began to grow and grow. Now they operate in some thirty-five countries— and it is young people, children who are doing this work. Craig is a Nobel Peace Prize nominee; he's now twenty-six. "Free the Children" now has 100,000 youth working in over thirty-five countries. The organization has built more than 400 primary schools, providing education to over 35,000 children every day. They've shipped 200,000 school and health kits around the world and have sent more than eight million U.S. dollars of medical supplies to help clinics in developing countries.

There is so much we can do—especially you, the younger people—when we're in touch with the reality of suffering in the world. We can look deeply into it, and when we create the space in our life to be present to that suffering, we can do so much to help. And the world really needs us to help—to help the planet, the animals and plant species.

Everybody in this hall is a Buddha. We all have the Buddha in us and we can't lose that no matter what happens, no one can take it away from us.

Let's sing together:

You are a Buddha
And you are in my heart
You are a part of me
You are a Buddha

You are the Dharma
And you are in my heart
You are a part of me
You are the Dharma

Let's look at each other when we sing.

You are the Sangha
And you are in my heart.
You are a part of me.
You are the Sangha .

You are so beautiful.
And you are in my heart.
You are a part of me.
You are so beautiful.

S H A R I N G S

Rachel Stansberry

All of what Thay is, is contained in all the non-Thay elements. In Colorado, I watched the Sangha sit and eat and work with a strength I hadn't seen before. I started to understand how we couldn't rely solely on the teacher to give us what we needed. We each have to find the Buddha in ourselves and to see the Buddha in each other. The Dharma in Colorado came from the monks and nuns who spoke each day, from the sitting, the walking, and the eating, and from the beautiful meadow in the morning where I could watch the clouds teach on impermanence. When I returned home, I couldn't say to my friends that Thay wasn't there.

Present in Thay's Absence by Lucy Mail

I am a Buddhist at heart but I'm not a disciplined practitioner. I come to the retreats every year to listen and see our dear Thay. In 2005, when I first heard Thay speak, he broke my heart and then put it back together with his words, compassion, and wisdom. Since then, my practice has been to do what Thay asks of me. I joined a Sangha; I use the skills he taught me to live in harmony with my significant other; I practice compassion with my coworkers and my patients, and during the retreats I try to move as one with the Sangha. During the YMCA retreat in Colorado, I worried about Thay's health to the degree that I was almost unable to participate in meditations or Dharma talks without breaking down. I realized at this retreat that everything I have done in my practice has been to please my teacher and not to find my own way. Thay's absence helped me realize this. His teachings were very present even in his absence.

Every Waking Moment by Mariann Taigman

I was so excited at the thought of being in the presence of Thay for the first time. I knew that it would be a unique and loving experience. I had made a beaded pouch that I was hoping to place in Thay's hands as a gift, in gratitude for all that he had taught me over the years and for opening his heart to all of us.

When I heard Thay would not be there, I decided that I would give the beaded pouch to one of the monks or nuns to give to Thay. I made a vow to myself that first night that I was going to "be in the moment" every moment during the retreat and experience it all for what it was, however it unfolded.

It was my first retreat, and what an amazing, wonderful, peaceful, and loving journey I had the pleasure of experiencing! It was six of the best days of my life, with the exception of the day I met my soul mate and best friend, who also happens to be my husband. I found myself frequently gazing at the altar and the beautiful words, "One Buddha Is Not Enough." All of us were there to help expand that statement.

The effects of the retreat have stayed with me. I work with children with special needs, and I had a meeting recently with two parents, their attorney, and the school district team. I was stressed about the meeting and that morning, I did a sitting meditation and a walking meditation. I practiced mindful walking as I approached the building where the meeting was being held, and watched my breath.

The meeting started out with some friction, but then it transformed. I focused on watching my breath go in and out. When it was my turn to talk, I realized that I was talking slower than I normally do and was much more thoughtful before speaking than I ever have been before. This is the magic of the Sangha, Thay's teachings, and my daily practice!

Many Buddhas in the Bell
by Michele McCormick

Dear Thay,

When I walked into the meditation hall that second morning of the retreat and encountered one thousand people sitting in silent meditation, I felt peace. I was relieved to have finally arrived, and to be home.

I did not pick up any signs of your absence, not that night or the next morning during the mindfulness walk. Instead, what I experienced was a deep relief as I entered a loving, alive, gentle, compassionate community. Truly, Thay, I thought you were here, resting somewhere in your lodge room, breathing in the beauty of the mountains, preparing to teach the wisdom of One Buddha Is Not Enough. I was shocked when, during the second Dharma talk, the sister teaching on Saturday morning referred to your absence almost in passing. I barely caught it because your presence was everywhere.

My ancestors are in these mountains,
these clouds,
this precious bowl of land and sky.

You see, I have come to the "why"... or the "Y"
since I was five years old. I am now 53.
So, when I touch the earth here, in this place,
at the YMCA, I *have* arrived, I *am* home.

My mother taught me to love nature.
My father taught me to sing, and
You, Thay, have shown me that I AM everything.

Thay, you are my Father,
you are my Mother.
You are in me, and I am in you.
And, We, the Sangha, are the breath-in-the-breath,
the many Buddhas in the Bell,
as we breathe with you.

Thay...
May we breathe *with* you,
may we breathe *for* you,
until we are *all* together
the wild and gentle dancing wind—

the wide open sky,
the granite peaks,
until our tears become rain,
and we are again
pebbles in the stream.

Until, when, we lie prone upon holy ground
and enter the Great Wheel beyond time and space,
we are *much* more than stardust.
We *have* arrived, we *are* home.

8: Go as a River

Brother Phap Niem

WHEN I WAS young, I learned how to sit like the Buddha, with a straight back and my knees touching the ground. When you have sadness, anger, irritation, sometimes the best thing to do is to find a place to sit down in this beautiful and solid position. When we are sad, we can go back to our mindful breathing. We put our hand on our belly and feel the rising and falling of our abdomen. Breathing in, I know that the Buddha is breathing with me. Breathing out, I smile to the Buddha and the Buddha smiles to me. Do you think that the Buddha is there with you? I find him in my mindful breathing.

This is a story of two rabbits. These two rabbits were born in a forest. When they were still very young, there was a fire in the forest. They tried to run away to safety with their family. But on the way, they lost their parents. So the older sibling, who was one year old, and the younger one, who was five or six months old, had to live together and help each other to survive and grow up. The elder one had to take care of the younger one. He knew how to run fast, how to dig a hole, how to make a house, and how to get food. So the elder rabbit taught his young brother how to do all of this so that when he grew up, he could survive by himself. They really loved and cared for each other. They had a lot of fun together. They ran and played in the fields, and enjoyed the beautiful flowers, trees, and mountains.

One day, when they went out to play, they saw a hunter sitting in the field in the green grass, eating his lunch. The rabbits saw he had a carrot—the favorite food of rabbits! They had never seen a carrot before, but somehow they knew it was the best kind of food. So they waited. They wanted to get the carrot, but they didn't know how. The hunter had a bow and arrow and he also had a gun; if they weren't careful they'd be killed and barbecued. So they had to wait for the hunter to take a nap.

The elder rabbit made a plan. He said to the younger one, "I'll stay here and you sneak up, okay? When I say 'left,' you go left. When I say 'right,' you go right. When I say 'take it,' you take it. When I say 'run,' you run, okay?" So the young one agreed. He sneaked in, came close to the hunter, and tried to get the carrot. When he came close, the hunter turned toward him. Wow, that was scary! The elder one said: "Lie down." And the young one lay down and hid in the grass so the hunter wouldn't see him. Then the hunter fell asleep and began to snore very loudly. While the hunter napped, the young rabbit continued to come closer, and closer, and finally he got the carrot. Wow! Lots of joy! He closed his eyes and he ran and ran and ran, really fast, faster than the best runner in the world! Then the elder ran after him, and they ran really, really, really fast, deep into the forest, until they came to a giant tree.

When they came to the big tree, do you know what happened? They fought over the carrot. They argued. Each of them wanted to have a bigger portion of the carrot instead of dividing it equally. The elder one said, "I deserve to get the big portion of the carrot, because I made the plan, I used my brain." And the younger one said, "But I risked my life to go there and get the carrot. If the hunter had woken up it would have been me who was killed, not you." And they continued to argue. The elder one said, "You know, I trained you how to run fast, do you remember? I trained you how to dig a hole to make a house. I did a lot of good things for you, so you should do something in return. If I hadn't made the plan and given you instructions, you wouldn't have known what to do." They continued to argue like that.

Do you children argue at home? Yes? I think the adults do too, but I'll ask them later. What things do you normally argue about? Television? One child said she sometimes argues with her dad about what program to watch, and she argues with her mom about what to wear to school. I remember when I was young, I fought with my sister over an ice cream. My sister was the youngest so my mom gave her an ice cream, but she didn't give me one. We were very poor so we rarely had candy or ice cream. I asked my sister, "Can't you give me a bite? Please!" And she said: "No! It's mine." I said, "I just want to taste it, please." She said, "No! No!" But then finally she gave it to me, thinking that I was only going to taste it. But instead, I took a big bite out of it! She cried and cried and cried, "Mom! He took all my ice cream!" And my mom yelled at me.

So the two rabbits were caught in this fighting because they'd lost something—they didn't remember that they were brothers. Suddenly a voice came down from the big tree. When they looked up, they saw an old monkey. This monkey looked very wise, but you have to be careful, you can't be sure. He sat up there and said, "You two rabbits! I've seen everything. I know that both of you deserve to have an equal portion of the carrot. You both contributed to the work of getting the carrot, you both deserve to share it in equal amounts, fifty-fifty. I can help you to make it fifty-fifty."

So the monkey tried to convince the two rabbits to let him help. He tried to fool them by talking sweetly and saying they both had worked hard and deserved an equal portion of the carrot, and that he would help them to do that. The monkey sounded very reasonable, so the rabbits agreed to give him the carrot to divide in half for them. Do you know why they gave it to him? Because when the rabbits got angry at each other, they lost all their intelligence and wisdom.

The monkey said, "I'm going to help you now. I have to use a scale. But even with this accurate method of weighing, sometimes one side is heavier than the other side. So I'll have to take off a piece to make it even. And that little piece will be for me, because I'm working, I'm helping you, so I deserve to have a piece too."

He broke the carrot in two and he put each piece on the scale. One side was a little heavier, so he broke a piece off that side. The rabbits continued to look at him, waiting to get their equal portion of carrot. And do you know what happened? In the end, there was no carrot left!

This monkey is there, he is everywhere. He is in our heart, he is around us; he is always there to bring us suffering when we're not mindful. The rabbits had never gone to a retreat to learn, they'd never had that chance like we do, to learn about the insight of inter-being. Do you know what the insight of interbeing is? I'm going to show you; it's very easy to understand.

I couldn't find a carrot but I found an apple to bring. I think rabbits like apples too. So let us explore this apple. If you can see the true nature, something hidden behind this apple, then you'll see the Buddha is in the apple too, just like the Buddha is in the bell. So let's do an exercise. Here's the apple. What else do you see in the apple? Sunshine, rain, hard work, water, soil, the farmer, trees, leaves, snow. (In Vietnam we can't grow apples, it's too hot!) What else do you see? Seeds, the universe, flowers. You see a lot of different things in the apple, and that is the insight of interbeing. This apple cannot *be* without all the things that we've mentioned. The apple cannot be without rain, without sunshine, without snow, without soil, without you, without me. If I'm not here and you are not here, the apple will not be here. This apple is here because I am here and you are there, and everything else is there as well. So when you see the apple in that way, you see the Buddha.

A long time ago at a retreat at the Omega Institute in New York, I heard a song the children sang which said the Buddha is even poo-poo. This is very hard for Asian Buddhists to accept. They feel the Buddha should be someone very beautiful and pure, and not like cow dung or poop. But in the insight of interbeing, the Buddha is made of non-Buddha elements, just like this apple is made of non-apple elements. If you take the sunshine out, if you take the farmer out, the soil out, the water out, if you take me away from this hall, and if I take you away from this hall, then this apple would not be here. So it is the Buddha. When you have that insight, you know that not only the apple is like that, but that you are the same, right? You are made of non-you elements. You are made of your brother and your brother is made of you. You are made of your sister and your sister is made of you. If you removed your brother, you wouldn't be the same person. You are there because your mom is there. If your mom wasn't there, you wouldn't be there, right?

Yesterday one of the children asked, "How can you meet your grandma if she died before you were born?" For me, when I look at my mom, I know my grandmother. My mom is the bridge for me to get in touch with my grandmother. If my mom were not there, I wouldn't have that chance. Sometimes when my mom cooks a dish, I ask her, "How do you know how to cook this dish, it's so delicious." My mom tells me: "Oh! It's from my mom, your grandmother." When you are mindful and you are there with the food while you eat, if you enjoy the dish you should ask your mom where it came from. Your mom is the continuation of your grandma.

In the insight of interbeing, you and your mom inter-are. If your mom was not there then there could be no daughter or son. If there's no son or daughter, how can a mom be a mom? A daughter is there because the mother is there. And the mother is there because the daughter is there. That is the insight. If the two rabbits could have this insight, they would love each other and they wouldn't fight over the carrot but would enjoy the carrot together. And the monkey wouldn't be able to take the carrot away. So be careful! Next time when you fight with your brother or sister, say to each other: "Be careful of the monkey!" And when you see your mom and dad fighting or arguing about something, say, "Mom, Dad, I see the monkey sitting there, be careful!" And then they'll know what to do. They'll stop fighting and arguing about this and that.

Can you see the Buddha in the bell now? Can you see the Buddha in the apple? Can you see the Buddha in you? Please continue to meet the Buddha, in the apple, in the flower, in you, in your mom, in everything that you see in your daily life.

The story about the rabbits is also my koan. It helps me to look deeply, to see the nature of interbeing, and to see that because of misunderstanding and ignorance, we don't see each other's true nature, and we don't see that everything in life is interbeing with everything else. Therefore we fight, we argue, we create suffering for each other and that's why wars and conflicts happen in the world, in our family, in school, in relationships. We fight to succeed in being equal. But to be equal in that way is a complex, just like a superiority complex or an inferiority complex. And because it's a complex, it creates suffering. In Buddhism we also talk about equality but it should always be seen in the light of interbeing, of nonself. The Buddha said that we are born equal because we share the same Buddha nature. Buddha nature is the nature of interbeing, of nonself, of interdependence, and so on.

If we don't have this insight, then even if we say we're equal, our idea of equality will continue to make us suffer. If the husband goes out to work and the wife stays home with the children, they're equally important. If the mother doesn't stay home to take care of the children, who will take care of them? In Vietnamese culture we don't use the words "you" and "I," "me" and "mine" so much. We say, "we." We use a much more community-minded kind of language. When I arrived in the meditation hall this morning, I saw a little piece of card saying "How are we doing?" It's a very good way to express concern.

One day the Buddha went before the assembly to give a Dharma talk to the monks, nuns, and laypeople. The Buddha held up a flower. He held it up for a long, long time and never said a word. After a long time of holding up the flower, only one person smiled and understood the message. I think there might have been many more, but in the sutra it said only the Venerable Mahakasyapa got the message. The Buddha smiled at Mahakasyapa, the elder brother in the community, and the Buddha said, "Mahakasyapa has the Dharma eye." And that was it; the Dharma talk was over.

With our ordinary eyes we see things as separate; we see things in the historical dimension. We see the apple as the apple; the apple cannot be the sun, the rain, or the snow. We see things as being outside of each other. But the Venerable Mahakasyapa was mindful and concentrated enough, his mind was clear, and he was able to touch the true reality of the flower, and of the Buddha. I've always thought that if the other people didn't get the message, it was because they were there, longing, waiting for the Buddha to say something. So their minds were busy, not completely silent.

When we're in the meditation hall, we may seem to sit there, still and solid, but in our heart there may be a lot of things going on, "What is Thay is going to say?" "Is he going to address something that concerns me?" Sometimes in the Dharma talk we think Thay is saying something directly to us, and we suffer because we think he's picking on us. And then someone else will say, "Oh! Thay gave that Dharma talk just for me." We come to the Dharma talk not with an open mind, but full of our thoughts, and so we aren't able to receive the deep teaching, even when we listen to Thay's teaching over and over again. Sometimes we feel, "Oh, he's repeating, I've heard that already, I want something new!" But if you're listening with the ears of Mahakasyapa, looking with the eyes of Mahakasyapa, you can see Thay in his ultimate dimension. You will see that there is the presence of a teacher, the presence of the Buddha, the presence of the Vietnam War in Thay's heart and in Thay's insight. There are a lot of things in Thay and we have to go beyond the words to get in touch with the true nature of Thay. If we come with our heart already full of things, it's impossible to get in touch with the true reality of the moment.

In our daily life we need to practice to produce the Dharma eye so we can see things as they are. Sister Dang Nghiem said that when we're walking and we see a flower, we think, "Oh I know that flower." Or when we come into the dining hall and see an orange, we think, "Oh I know that orange." But maybe not! It may be just a name, an appearance, and not the real orange because we don't see its interbeing nature. We have to look deeply, to break through the outer form of the orange, to see the true nature of the orange. Normally, we don't see in that way; we look with our ordinary eyes and we see that the orange is different from the apple, that I am different from you, that husband is different from wife, that son is different from daughter, and that is why we suffer.

In the Diamond Sutra it says that when your mind is not attached to anything then the beautiful mind of nondiscrimination will be born. When our mind is not attached to any particular form, sight, appearance, then we can see the Buddha. When the rabbits were full of anger, desire, and discrimination, they weren't able to see that although they're two, they are one—they coexist, they interare—and that's why they lost the carrot. The monkey represents the self, the discriminating mind, and the monkey is always there saying things like, "Oh, you're good and she's bad," or "You do a lot and he is just lazy." There's a lot of talking going on inside us when we look at things, when we say things, and it creates suffering. So we have to train ourselves to be mindful, to continually nourish the insight of nonself and interbeing in order to be free from the notion of self so we can bring happiness, love, and compassion to ourselves, each other, and the world.

Thay once told the story of a little girl in Italy. When her little sister was born, she became jealous. Her little sister seemed to get all the love, attention, and care from her parents. The big sister had to share all the attention with her younger sister. Her mom and dad paid more attention to the baby and she felt neglected. She didn't feel she had enough love from her parents and she was attached to the love they'd given her before. She was jealous of her younger sister. She even had the thought that she'd like her little sister to die so she could have all her parents' love again. And she held on to this idea for three or four years, until she was able to come to a retreat.

Sometimes when a couple has their first child, it can be a struggle. The wife gives all her time and attention to the baby, and the husband feels left out or the couple feels they have no time for each other. I've met couples like that in Plum Village. But they know how to practice to overcome it. They know that taking care of the child is also taking care of themselves and each other. Taking time to be there for the child is also taking time to be there for themselves and each other—because the child is their continuation. This little girl didn't yet have that insight, and she suffered. But luckily, she and her family came to a retreat, and Thay taught the children how to get in touch with the insight of interbeing, using the image of the olive trees that he'd seen that year in Italy.

Driving along a road, Thay noticed many olive trees with three or four trunks. A few winters before, the weather had been so cold that it seemed the olive trees had died, so the farmers cut them down. But under the earth, the roots were still alive. And when the spring came, three or four new trunks came up where only one had been before. There were three trunks, but they were the same tree. Thay used that image to teach the children to see that they were born from the same ground as their siblings, that they inter-are with each other. They share the same mother and father, so they're branches of the same tree. If you cut one branch the others feel it too. It's like our five fingers; if one finger is hurt, the other fingers also feel the pain. During the retreat something transformed in the little girl and she began to love her little sister. It's amazing. She removed the thought of wishing her sister wasn't there so she could get all the love from her parents.

The teaching of the Buddha is very beautiful and very deep. I have been practicing for fifteen years, and I continue to learn more. The more I learn and practice, the more I see how beautiful it is. Every morning and evening before reciting a sutra or another text, we say: "The Dharma is deep and lovely."

When we don't have the insight of interbeing and nonself, then our mind functions on the basis of self. We discriminate and see things as being outside of each other. Last year, I helped lead a retreat in Hanoi, in the north of Vietnam. There was a woman who had consultation with me. She was suffering a lot because of her son. He was tall, handsome, and well-educated; he'd gone to England to study at Oxford University. He'd met a young woman from Da Nang, in the center of Vietnam. She and the young man loved each other very much and they wanted to get married. But the mother could not accept it, because the young woman was short and had dark skin. The mother told me: "My son is handsome, intelligent, and beautiful and he's too good for that young woman. Also the culture is different, the way of living is different in the South." But she couldn't convince her son, and she was worried that if she objected too strongly, she would lose her son.

So she held the suffering for a long time, and she got very ill. She couldn't sleep and she had to take sleeping pills. But still she couldn't sleep, and she became very weak and she developed another illness. I told her, "You should let go of your notion, of your idea, of your discriminatory mind, and allow your son to get married to the one he loves the most. You are the mother and the mother should be able to bring happiness to the children. But if you are caught in discriminating mind, in notions of self and other, of family and cultural

differences, then you suffer and you'll make your son suffer, and you may lose him. Have you ever sat down and listened to your son?" The mother cried and said, "I wonder what the people around me will think of me for allowing my son to marry such a young woman." This was a pressure on her as well. I talked to her about various practices for letting go of the discriminative mind. I told her she should try to sit down with him and talk, and she agreed. And I said, "The moment you let go of that discriminating mind, your illness will be healed." Later on I found out she'd gotten much better and had accepted the marriage of her son to the young woman. So as parents, when we dwell with the insight of interbeing, of nonself, of nondiscrimination, we can bring a lot of happiness to our children.

The Diamond Sutra says there are four kinds of notions we need to remove in order to be free and truly happy. The first notion is that of self. Look into the apple. The apple is full of everything. There is only one thing the apple doesn't contain, and that is a separate self.

Before coming here to give the talk, my brothers and sisters asked me: "Who will be there to give the talk with you?" I said, "Me and my ultimate dimension." When you look up here, you see me, but you don't see the others who are sitting here with me. I am the form, the others are emptiness. But emptiness is form. Thay is sitting here in his ultimate dimension. If you look at me, at the other monks and nuns, if you look at yourself, Thay is there. If you run away from me, from the monks and nuns, from yourself, you will not see the true existence of Thay. There is no self. There is the nature of interbeing—it's in me, in you, in the flower, in the loudspeaker, it's in all of us. If there's no "me" here, then Thay cannot be here also. And if there's no Thay, then I cannot be here. Thay is a teacher and I am a student. A teacher needs a student to manifest as a teacher, and a student needs a teacher in order to be called a student. Although Thay is not here in his physical appearance, he is here in his ultimate dimension. I don't contain a self, I inter-am with Thay, I inter-am with you, I inter-am with my brothers and sisters. When the brothers and sisters sit up here to give a Dharma talk, I feel I'm also sitting up here with them; I don't feel any kind of complex.

Self is a notion. Can we find anything that exists by itself alone? No. The idea of self is a prison that locks us up. Self is one of the notions that imprisons us every day and every night. An image that I like very much is the Chinese character for "great." Great here doesn't mean you do something good. Great here means the cosmos. I, you, we are the cosmos. Inside of me and inside of you, you can find everything, your mom, your dad, your ancestors, the mountains, the rivers, the Buddha, Jesus Christ, God, Mohammed, everything. But most of the time we don't see that we are everything; we think that we are someone manifesting separately from everything else. We think that we are not our mom, we are not our grandma. So self is the first of the four notions. The other three notions are the notions of human being, living being, and life span. Each of them is also a prison, four walls that trap us when we're not able to open ourselves and connect to the ultimate.

So our practice is to remove our notions of self and to see that self is made of nonself elements; that is the teaching of nonself. If I know how to do something well, it is not about me, it's my ancestors. Before Thay gives a Dharma talk I normally begin the chant and then the monks and nuns join in with me. Afterward, when I walk outside, people come up and say: "Oh! You sang so beautifully." If I'm caught in my self then I feel, "Yeah! Great! It's my accomplishment." But I try to practice and say, "Oh, thank you. That is because of my ancestors." Thay is always reminding me of that. Once when I was traveling with Thay, he reminded me, "You know, son, that is not your voice." And I answer, "Yes, Thay." I know that my mom chants very well, so my mom transmitted that quality to me. So the voice that I have, it has my ancestors' voices in it; I'm only the continuation. I don't have anything in me that is only me. If a basketball star makes a basket, it's not about that one player. That shot is the product of the team. If there's no defense, then the player can't receive the pass and make a basket. So the basket depends on the whole team, not just a basketball star. If the basketball star sees that, he will be safe. If he doesn't, he will get caught in the ego, in the self.

The second notion is that of human being. Can human beings exist by themselves alone? No. Humans inter-are with other things: the animals, plants, and minerals. If we think God created all the other things only for humans to enjoy, to kill, and to eat, then we're caught in the notion of human being. Humans cannot be by themselves alone. Humans need to inter-be with everything else. We know that to survive we need the water, the mountains, the trees, the air, and the minerals to be there so that we can be. If we kill and destroy the animals, the plants, the land, the minerals, then we destroy ourselves. So, in order to be truly compassionate and truly free, we need to remove this notion of human being.

The third notion is that of living being—of living beings being something separate from so-called non-living beings. If we know how to look deeply with the insight of interbeing and nonself, we know that everything is interconnected. The so-called living beings are also made of non-living being elements. We learn to be humble, to love, respect, and be compassionate with all beings.

The fourth notion is that of life span. By removing this notion, we can remove a lot of fear in ourselves. We touch the no-birth and no-death nature of reality. We transcend the notions of coming and going, being and non-being. I am standing up here, but at the same time I'm sitting down there with you. And I'm also outside, in other forms of life. I'm a tree. If the trees were not there, I wouldn't have oxygen to breathe. If there were no oxygen, I would collapse.

When someone we love dearly dies, we think that person is gone, and he or she is no longer there. That is not true. We are the continuation of our ancestors, our parents, and our friends. Our parents are here with us. In Vietnamese, there is a saying, "Wherever the children are, the ancestors are." It's just like wherever the left is, the right is. If we split this marker in different sections and if we take away the left section, the section that was next to it becomes the left.

Recently, I was in Vietnam. While I was there, the Bat Nha monastery, home to almost 400 monastics, was attacked for the first time. Many of us wanted to be there to help take care of the problem and be a strong support for our younger brothers and sisters. One day, I received the very painful news from my family in Canada that my nephew, Tony, had been in an accident and was in a coma. I was torn.

I needed to be at Bat Nha to support my Sangha, which was being attacked. On the other hand, my nephew was in a coma and he was dying. My brother-in-law called me and he couldn't say a word. He gave the phone to his son, the younger brother of the one who'd been in the accident. This young one was very solid, though he was only fifteen. He was able to be calm enough to tell me what had happened to Tony. It was a sad news, painful news. I went to my room and lit a stick of incense. I sat down and I went back to my breathing and I looked deeply into my nephew to see the true nature of his suffering.

When I lit the incense I suddenly remembered a time I walked with Thay on a path in Plum Village. Thay was spreading the ashes of a lay student who had lived in Plum Village for many years. He had died in the U.S. but he wanted his ashes to be spread in Plum Village. I walked with Thay while he spread the ashes and I held the incense. After he'd finished, Thay and I went back to the hut. We washed our hands and then we sat down for tea. Thay asked me the question, "What do you think when you hold the incense like that?" I was silent for a bit, and then I said, "I see that the incense is just like Jim," the friend who died. "Jim has lived his life and he has shared his beauty, his love, his care, his understanding with many other people. So he is already reborn into many forms of life."

When we light a stick of incense, if we look at it deeply, the incense will teach us a lot. The smoke will be transformed into a cloud and continue its life as a cloud. The heat of the incense penetrates into our body and becomes part of ourselves. The fragrance penetrates into the room and many other people enjoy the fragrance, and it also becomes part of everything around it. And what is left is the ash, and that ash, we think it's dead, but it's not dead. Ash is also a form of life. Nothing is dying, life is just transforming into something else, and it's just playing a game of hide and seek. When I hold up this flower, you can see the flower in front of me, but if I put it behind my back, you may think it's no longer there—that's how we see birth and death with our ordinary eyes. But the flower is still there, behind me.

I looked into the incense and I meditated. I saw that my nephew is always there, in me, in my brother-in-law, in my sister, in his brother, in his sister, and in the monks and nuns too, because Tony had visited all the monasteries of Thay, even those in Vietnam, and he had met many beautiful monks and nuns and he loved them so much. He got into an accident on his eighteenth birthday. There was a birthday celebration organized at home. He and his friend were in the bathroom together, and he didn't know that his friend had a gun. They were playing with the gun and Tony got shot. Tony's brain was severely damaged. He was brought to the hospital, and the doctors tried for many days to save him, but they couldn't. Everything was still alive, only the brain was not functioning. He needed to breathe with a respirator.

Finally the doctor told my brother that he could survive but only in this way, brain dead. They suggested that we unplug everything so

Tony could go. In our culture, if people die naturally, it's sad but it's okay. But to do something to make someone die, it's a very difficult decision. So my sister asked me over the phone if we should do it. I said that it's something we can do, but not now. Just leave it for a few days and we can guide him. So I asked my brothers, my sister, and my nephew who know the practice well to sit around him, give him massage, and talk to him. People who are in a coma can still hear; they can still receive the love, the care, and the words from us.

In Buddhist psychology, there is the mind consciousness and there is the store consciousness. And there's another consciousness called *manas*. According to Buddhist psychology, the store consciousness and manas are working day and night; even if you're in a coma, they're still working and functioning. But mind consciousness can shut down and stop working. But the other two consciousnesses continue to work. Consciousness can be found in every cell of our body; scientists have discovered that to be true. So when we send loving, compassionate, peaceful energy to our loved one who is in a coma, all the cells of the body can receive it because the store consciousness and manas continue to receive and transform.

Tony's younger brother, who was then fifteen, had come to Plum Village when he was ten and during that time he'd asked Thay a question: "Dear Thay, how can I become a Buddha?" And Thay said, "It's easy! Be mindful." So he had received the practice, and he was the one in the family who was very solid and strong and who helped in any situation. He was in the room and he guided Tony with wonderful words. Everybody came. They felt sad, some were crying, and some were almost crying. He gathered all of Tony's young friends as well as all the relatives, even the elder ones, to sit around him and meditate and send peaceful, solid, non-fear energy to Tony. Then others continued to talk to Tony. And suddenly Tony moved his fingers and toes, but his mind was still not working. My sister shared a lot of wonderful things about him, and so did my brothers and Tony's friends. And then a few days later, Tony decided to go naturally. His face was very peaceful. My brother and sister didn't need to take the tubes out, which was wonderful for them. If they'd had to do that, they would have suffered later on. They themselves were okay with it, but they were afraid that other people would say differently.

John wrote a beautiful eulogy for his older brother. Part of it read:

"A few days ago my cousin Quoc gave a great speech. He said you shouldn't wait to express your feelings for someone you love, and we should be able to get the family to gather together without first having to lose someone. I never told Tony I love him, so I hope it's not too late to tell you this now: Tony, you were nothing less than perfect; you always tried to help me when I needed it, through the bad times and the good times. I will always love you and you will always be in my heart, even though you're gone. I don't feel you are actually gone.

The other day when I was looking for your suit with Thien, my knee hurt. I usually have good knees but you had always had pain in your knees. Kneeling there, I felt like I was experiencing your pain in my own body. I love you, and you will always be with me. I wish you the best of luck in the afterlife, and may you rest in peace."

John was only fifteen when he wrote this eulogy and he was able to see the nature of no birth and no death of his elder brother. I think that all of us are capable of seeing our true nature of no birth and no death. Our life span is not only eighteen years, thirty, sixty, or seventy years. Our life span is much longer. We were there before we were born; we were there in our mother and our father and our ancestors. When someone dies, it does not mean that person is gone. It's like the way John experienced Tony always being there, in him, in his mother and father, in me, in the trees, in the mountains, in the rivers. He manifests in countless forms of life. That is our true nature. And when we see that, we remove the last notion, the notion of life span. And we go back to our true existence. We become great and we're connected to everything around us and we see that we are part of everything else. That is the insight of no birth and no death.

SHARINGS

Brother Phap Trien

When we arrived in Denver, I could feel the crisp thin air going through my lungs. It felt good to be back in Colorado. I learn a lot by traveling with the Sangha. I learn to "go as a river," as Thay likes to say. I remember having lunch at the baggage claim. We were enjoying every second with each other. Whenever I eat like that with my blood family I feel embarrassed somehow, but with the Sangha I don't get the feeling of embarrassment. My time before, during, and after the retreat was a great time for me to get to know the brothers and sisters from Blue Cliff and Deer Park. I think that is one of the things that I value most about Colorado.

After we had a whole day to play and to go hiking, we had our first Sangha meeting. I was kind of nervous because I didn't have any responsibilities for the retreat since I am usually Thay's attendant. So I came in with no responsibilities, and I came out with the children's program. This was the last thing I wanted to do, but I volunteered because they needed help there. It turned out that being with the children was one of the best things I could have done. I learned so much about myself. I thought that the children would be very annoying and loud. At times they were annoying and loud, but I embraced it. I thought I would never be able to embrace and say "hi" to my anger.

My children's group was named the Laughing Elks. The children nicknamed me "Boo," which is slang for my dear friend. At first I didn't really like it, but I saw the kids enjoyed calling me Boo, so I stuck with it. I really enjoyed being with the children. They shared very deeply and it nourished me a lot. At the end of the retreat we transmitted the Two Promises to the children. It was a very emotional ceremony and I was remembering when Thay had transmitted the Two Promises to me. I wouldn't trade my experience with the children for anything.

Kathy Bednark

My image of the retreat was the thistle—the beauty and the thorns. That is absolutely how it is. I will never have one without the other in myself—nor will anyone else. It is not just sweetness and light, this journey we are on. It's also about recognizing and dealing with the not so pleasant stuff, the negative seeds that can seem to take on a life of their own.

One Rock Star Is Not Enough
by Angelina Chin

When I arrived the first evening and realized that Thay was not there, I was very disappointed and felt cheated. I even told one friend that it was as if I had gone to a rock concert but the rock star had bailed out!

I was a night owl, so I couldn't fall asleep on my first night, and by the time I finally felt sleepy it was time to get up to do walking meditation. It was very difficult for me to keep up with the activities of the first two days. Because of the lack of sleep, I slept through the Dharma talks. And while many of the Sangha members found the food to be quite decent, I wasn't used to a vegan diet and didn't enjoy it during the first two days. Of course I practiced eating meditation, but the more I meditated, the more I thought about the food I enjoyed outside the retreat. I also formed negative perceptions of some Sangha members.

I'm not exactly sure what happened to me in the following days, but gradually I found myself enjoying every moment of the retreat. I think the wonderful songs were a great help. It was very healing to be able to sing and practice with a Sangha of nearly a thousand people. Everyone was so friendly, focused, and happy. It was very comforting to me, especially because I grew up in a different cultural environment and always have felt racial and gender discrimination around me. Toward the end of the retreat I became quite mindful. The food became tastier. Before the retreat I had only known Thay's works by their titles, but his teachings really sank in during the retreat.

After a few days I began to realize that Thay's physical absence was a good lesson in itself. It had been so silly of me to compare the retreat to a rock concert. I'd attended the retreat to practice mindfulness, not to look for the rock star! I think because Thay was not there, the members were less attached to his presence and became more focused on the practice itself. I did feel Thay's spiritual presence, and I missed him very much. But I also want to express my gratitude to the monastic brothers and sisters who tried so hard to make the retreat possible. It must have been a great deal of pressure on them. I could totally see both the Buddha and Thay in all of them! Thank you, Thay, for training our future teachers.

I received the Five Mindfulness Trainings on the last day. I hadn't planned to do so, but since the day after the retreat was my birthday and I wanted to celebrate my rebirth and show my commitment to becoming more mindful, I decided to receive them. I also was given a beautiful Dharma name—Wonderful Fragrance of the Heart. I felt peaceful when I left Colorado.

Here are a few of the ways my life has changed since the retreat:

- I had insomnia before, and couldn't get up until around 10:00 A.M. Now the insomnia has been cured and I wake up at seven every morning.
- I practice walking meditation every day.
- I've cut down my meat and seafood consumption by 40%. I've also decided not to cook meat at home.
- I try not to kill any living beings.
- I can concentrate much better at meetings.
- I've practiced Beginning Anew with friends. These friendships are now better than ever. I will continue to listen to them with my heart.
- I used to have an inferiority complex, which had been affecting my life in many ways. Now I am more aware of my mental formations and try not to water my negative seeds. Life is more pleasant and I feel more confident and engaged.
- I've become less judgmental of others and have built new relationships.
- I drive more mindfully. I think I'm a safer driver now.
- I've witnessed some improvement in my meditation and breathing practices.
- Even though negative emotions still visit me frequently, I've learned to be patient and try my best to take care of them.

I was so inspired that I attended a Day of Mindfulness at Deer Park Monastery for the first time and finally met Thay! It was a blessing.

Prayer of Everyday Life
by Alexis Roberts

As in water, the glint of sunlight,
or the silent seasons of the moon,
our bodies carry memory. And longing.
Whether the Aboriginal bull roarers
swinging voices of the spirits
or the trance dances of Bushmen,
we look for the opening beyond ourselves
that we might touch the four elements,
bow to the four directions.

Put down the stories you carry.
They are not the stars burning through.
Let go the territory of self
or miss the single falling leaf.
Break through the urge to carve on trees
and freeze in your tracks,
holding like deer in the here, in the now.
Know what the wind is doing.
This is the burnished face of joy.

Be the heart of compassion, embrace yourself.
His eyes, her smile—
that pain, that joy, that fear—all yours.

There is no only me.
It is impossible to be lost.

Forget yourself in the footfall
of perfect experience.
Sanctify your belonging.
There is only one of us here.
Breathe for the sake of breathing.
Walk for the sake of walking,
gathering to yourself as comfort
a love that tumbles over itself.
The prayer of everyday life
is the peace and freedom
of not knowing beyond this moment.

i know you
are there and
i am very
happy

9: I Know You Are There and I Am Very Happy

Sister Thoai Nghiem and Brother Phap Ho

Beginning Anew by Sister Thoai Nghiem

TWELVE OR THIRTEEN years ago when I was in Plum Village, I had to do a lot of Beginning Anew with my sisters because we were young in the practice. We all have our own expectations and ways of seeing things, and we have the tendency to want other people to do things our way. So we have a lot of stories from the time we lived together.

In Plum Village we lived as an international Sangha. There were nuns from Europe, North America, Vietnam, and other countries. I had a Dharma sister from Germany who told me that fresh pineapple is very expensive and hard to find there. In Vietnam it's the cheapest fruit. Whenever we offered fruit to the Buddha in Plum Village, we'd normally buy three or four pineapples and combine them with apples and other fruits. After the offered fruits had been on the altar for a while, we'd bring them to the kitchen. On that day, a Vietnamese sister was cooking and my German sister was her cooking partner. With the language barrier, they didn't communicate very well. The cook thought, "Oh, pineapple is something very cheap and normally we make sour soup with it." So she cut up the pineapple and made soup. My dear German sister was busy with her own dish. She'd already spoken to the other sisters saying that we should save the fruits, and she'd planned to serve the fresh pineapple as dessert. But it was all gone, into the soup. Something as simple as that can make the sisters not very happy with each other. Then the misperceptions started to arise. The German sister thought the Vietnamese sisters didn't listen to her and did everything they wanted without consulting the cooking team. She began to be irritated and spoke a little less lovingly. The Vietnamese sister who was her teammate was surprised because she wondered, "What's the big deal about those pineapples?" So then we had to have Beginning Anew to renew the relationship between the two. Also the Vietnamese sisters like crunchy fruits. They like to pick pears when they aren't yet ripe and eat them with chili and salt. To the Western sisters, this may seem destructive because the fruits aren't ripe yet. This is an opportunity for another Beginning Anew.

When I went to Vietnam and lived in Bat Nha Monastery with two hundred other sisters, we practiced Beginning Anew right away. Even though all the sisters were Vietnamese, they were all quite different from each other. They came from the north, the south, and the center; some had lived in the city, some in rural areas, and they'd led very different lives. But because they were very new to the practice we asked them to do Beginning Anew often, at least once a week. They could do it with their roommates—we lived with about sixteen sisters in one room that was quite small. Each room was for four, but we filled it with bunk beds and we just had to stack people in because they kept coming and wanted to become monastics and we could not say no. Or they could do Beginning Anew as a cooking team—we had around ten people on a cooking team. Or they could do Beginning Anew as a working team with around twelve people on each working team. So there were all forms of Beginning Anew that they had to do all year long. With all of that, we lived quite happily and in quite good communication.

There's a funny story. There was one venerable nun who lived in Saigon, the largest city in the south of Vietnam, who had a temple with twenty nuns. She came to visit us and was quite surprised. She said, "I have only twenty nuns, but they quarrel and I always have to be the judge to solve their problems." So she asked whether she could bring all twenty nuns up to live with us for just three months. Of course we said, "Sure, please." After that I had to go back to France to obtain a new visa, and then I came back to Bat Nha. I

learned that the nuns had already come and, after some quarrels, left. When I heard that, I was so worried. I said, "You guys have been practicing so well for the whole year and then when we have guests, you quarrel! That does not present a good image." My young sister looked at me very naively and she said, "Don't worry big sister, they quarreled with each other!" It was true. When they lived with us, they still couldn't observe the new Dharma door and they couldn't practice. During that month, they argued quite a number of times and the venerable nun, feeling so hopeless, took her nuns back to her temple.

You know, in our daily life we encounter each other with a lot of misperceptions. Sometimes we see it with our own eyes, we hear it with our own ears, but things still aren't like what we think. I trust that everyone has experience with this! So when it happens, we need to do something to restore the communication. The way that we do this is with the practice of Beginning Anew.

Brother Phap Ho

Beginning Anew is the perfect practice for restoring communication and connection with our loved ones. Beginning Anew is to reconnect, to establish and build relationships with ourselves and with others, and to understand that we inter-are, that we're not separate, as we sometimes tend to think—that this is me and I'm cut off and separate from everyone else, so I'll just take care of me. But actually, we're so intertwined. When you look into a friend's eyes and you see the freshness, the clarity in their eyes, the smile on their face, it's already Beginning Anew happening, you feel refreshed, you have a chance to be open, connected.

I have a friend who has been attending the retreats at Deer Park for a couple of years, and who also has come on a couple of the trips to Vietnam with Thay and the Sangha. I met him in Hanoi last year where we had a retreat and attended a Buddha's birthday celebration; he was there and we shared some conversations. One day he approached me and he shared that just before coming to Vietnam, he had visited his parents. This man is in his sixties and his parents are in their late eighties, but there is still some difficulty in their relationship. They hadn't spoken for a long time, and when they had spoken, there'd been a lot of anger, a lot of separation, they hadn't felt connected.

He was sharing with me that he continued in his practice, that he had started writing letters to his parents and he started calling them, and just before the Vietnam trip he actually went to visit them for the first time in a couple of decades. Just looking at him when he was sharing this, his eyes and his face were so fresh, so renewed, at ease, like a little boy, maybe six, who's been out in the field playing with his father and feels so happy and nourished—very simple but very real. When we're able to connect with our parents, our siblings, our partner, our children, we feel alive and we're really touching life. That's a little bit what Beginning Anew is all about—finding a way to reconnect, to Begin Anew with ourselves, but also with our loved ones, with the people around us.

Another aspect of Beginning Anew is renewing oneself. I'm able to be open to the other person's goodness and beauty. When we come together, we cultivate our awareness, we come back to ourselves, we practice stopping, we don't let our emotions or our thoughts take us away and run our life, and we cultivate our capacity to come back, to be still, to be quiet. We don't just see the flowers from here, but we're able to discover and to investigate them, and not just have an idea about them: "This is a flower, it's called such and such." But we're seeing the life of the flower. We're able to connect with the smile, the freshness, the beauty of the flower.

There are many other things we can do to refresh ourselves. Sometimes when you're working on your computer, if there are too many applications running or something's not going well, you restart, right? So you know how to restart your computer. We can also restart or reboot ourselves. I remember when I was living and working in Stockholm, I was lucky enough to be within a ten-minute walk of a couple of parks. These parks were situated on hills, so you could be up on the hill with the trees and the plants and the birds but still see the city. I wasn't really aware of what was happening, but every time I went up there, I felt renewed and refreshed; it was kind of like a refuge. Without knowing it, I was drawn to this place because it opened me up, it helped me to let go of the stress from daily life, it helped me to let go of thinking of this and that, and it just helped me to stop. So, in our life we can investigate: What helps us to come back to ourselves, what really inspires us to come back and refresh? Another thing I enjoy doing is running. I live in Deer Park Monastery up in the mountains. After spending an hour or so up on the mountain doing a vigorous hike or running, I feel like a different person when I come down—my body, my mind are very different than when I started.

There are also other ways in our daily practice that help us to come back and to nourish the capacity and the trust that it's actually possible to see things in a new light. One of the lines of a meditation chant that the monks and nuns practice regularly goes: "This is a new day, I vow to go through it in mindfulness." We're not successful all the time at keeping this outlook, but little by little we cultivate that way of looking at life. Another way to practice is with this little poem when you first wake up:

Waking up this morning, I smile
Twenty-four brand new hours are before me
I vow to live deeply in each moment
And to look at all beings with eyes of compassion.

We may feel drowsy when we first say this and think: "Do I really have to get up now? It's too early; it's cold." Somehow just remembering that poem helps us see the moment differently. It can be quite wonderful to wake up and come out before the light and the sun has risen, before everything is up and going.

There's a story in the Lotus Sutra that talks about this great being, the Bodhisattva who is called Never Disparaging, Never Discouraging. This Bodhisattva goes around in life looking at everyone he or she meets and saying, "You are a Buddha-to-be. You have the Buddha capacity in you, and I see this nature in you." Is that what we recognize when we meet a new person? It can be.

Every summer in Deer Park we have a family retreat. I think we had four generations present at the last one. We practice Beginning Anew and we invite the children, teenagers, and adults to practice with us as a family. One family this past year had three sisters. They were all grown up, and one of the sisters had three daughters. In the Beginning Anew session, the two sisters that did not have children expressed how grateful they felt to their sister for taking refuge in them and allowing them to spend so much time with her daughters, their nieces. Each sister remembered how deep their connection was and how precious it is to have sisters. This kind of flower watering changes your perspective on things. It can become the foundation of your relationships.

The second practice of Beginning Anew is to express regret. Maybe we can call it "I'm sorry." Do you find it easy to say "I'm sorry" when you feel like you've made a mistake? It's interesting to look into this. Sometimes we bump into someone or we cut in front of someone in the grocery store or something, and it's "sorry" this, "sorry" that, but you haven't really done anything that created any suffering. We say sorry for this and that. The practice of expressing regret is more like saying, "I'm sorry, I recognize the way I spoke to you, I recognize it might have hurt you. I didn't mean to say it like that, and I hope I can be more skillful and kind in the future." I had an example of that just the other day. One morning I was in the administration building and there was a father and his young son walking into the men's room. The father said, "You know, when I said that this morning I felt like I was irritated. I'm really sorry. I didn't mean to say that." It was such a beautiful thing to hear. And the son said, "Okay, no problem." The father said this very shortly after the incident, and it allowed them to Begin Anew.

Many times we are in small situations in which we say things that hurt people we care about. We have the habit energy of blaming someone, talking in an irritated way, or judging the other person. These small hurts accumulate. Little by little, people don't trust us anymore. They don't feel seen and appreciated anymore because we don't tell them, "Thank you" or say, "I'm sorry."

When I first became a monk, I thought about the many relationships I've had with family and friends and partners, and I felt regret. I have a cousin who is two years older than me and we grew up together. We spent a lot of time with my grandparents, and somehow many times my grandparents blamed him for things we both did. He would take it out on me, tease me and hit me. We had a lot of fun together, we played a lot, but there was also this something that was not really in harmony. There were a couple of times in my grandparents' house that I broke something and I was too scared to tell them, especially my grandfather. So my cousin got the blame and was held responsible for things that I actually did.

When I became a monk, I wrote him a letter expressing my regret for that situation and that time. It was a release to acknowledge these actions that I wasn't proud of. Expressing my regret, I had a chance to transform these feeling and to Begin Anew, to reconnect.

The third aspect of Beginning Anew is putting down the burden. Suppose something stressful is happening—perhaps we have a new manager at work or someone we love is sick. When we're not in that stressful situation and we're with our family and friends, we can try to put down the stress and let it be. It may help to express what is happening and let them know what is difficult. Put your bags down. Arrive. The situation may not have changed, but if we're able to express it to someone, we'll be able to Begin Anew for ourselves.

We might have all kinds of ideas regarding our mother, our partner, our friend, why he or she is acting in a tight and unkind way to us. We might feel hurt and think we've done something wrong. We don't share about it, so we have all these ideas running in our mind. Beginning Anew is a wonderful way to express what is happening right then.

The fourth aspect of Beginning Anew is expressing hurt. We could call it "I suffer." When we're in a situation in which we've been hurt—perhaps we feel angry or jealous—we can come back to our own feelings and then try to be objective about how we describe that situation. What happened? What did the other person really do or say? Then we can express what we experienced in a constructive way, without blaming. When one person is expressing hurt, that person might speak based on a misperception. "The other day you did that to me and I really suffered." When you're the person who speaks first and who is expressing hurt, try to just recount the incident. Don't add your perception into that. You can add your feeling, "I feel so sad because you didn't look at me." Or "I feel so sad because I said hello and you didn't reply," but don't say, "I know that you look down on me and that's why when I said hello you didn't answer me." Try to avoid your perception, your interpretation. Most perceptions are misperceptions. Just express your feeling. The purpose of doing Beginning Anew is to re-establish the relationship. So if you love each other and you keep that in mind, you can do it.

Recently I met with a couple who has been practicing for years and has had some challenges in their relationship. They asked me and another monastic if they could come and practice Beginning Anew together with us. They were both working on their relationship and really wanted to learn and grow, but they had habit energies that triggered each other's anger and jealousy. They practiced expressing their feelings without blaming the other person and— very importantly—watered each other's flowers by appreciating each other. This couple was able to very beautifully express thank-yous and regrets. Once they started paying more attention and practicing Beginning Anew with intention, their relationship started to feel as if it was being nourished again.

When we do Beginning Anew more formally, we have a vase of flowers—one flower is also enough. If the Beginning Anew is between just two people, the flower will be in the middle. When it's my turn to speak, I bow and I put the flower in front of me. So long as I have the flower, I can speak and the other person has to do deep listening. And of course I have to practice loving speech, not accusing the other person. When I've finished speaking, I return the flower to the center. Then it's the other person's time to speak and it's time for me to listen. Especially when two people are having trouble and are doing Beginning Anew together, if it's really a serious matter, it's best not to try to speak back right away, but just to let one person speak. What that person says might have some truth in it, and our automatic reaction might be to say, "Oh, you've misunderstood me; that's not correct." But if you let it sink in for a while, maybe a couple of days, you might see some truth in it. Don't be in too much of a rush to defend yourself.

Questions and Answers

Sister Huong Nghiem, Brother Phap Dung, Brother Phap Tri, Sister Chau Nghiem, Rowan Conrad, and Cheri Maples

Child's Question: My question is "Why am I here?" I don't mean why am I here on the stage or in the retreat? I mean why am I me?

Brother Phap Dung: That's a wonderful question to keep asking yourself. Every moment, we should be asking that question. When we ask it deeply, we can really touch ourselves beyond what we look like as a boy or a girl. As we grow older, we might think that we know the answer. And that's what a lot of trouble comes from.

As a young person, you can ask your parents, "Mom, are you here? Dad, are you here?" When you sit on a cushion, you ask yourself, "Why am I here?" If you listen to yourself deeply enough, maybe you'll find out.

Sometimes we are not really here, right? Our mind is already thinking of something else. Sometimes that prevents us from listening, and so we miss out on a lot of things. We miss out on our loved ones. We think we're really there with them. But actually, we're not there, so they're not really there either. Sometimes you look at a flower, and you don't see the flower, you're already thinking about something else.

Where am I? Am I really here? What am I doing here? When I ask these questions, they bring me back to the present moment. "I know where I am, I'm here. How lucky I am that I'm still alive, young, and growing." Keep asking that question: "What am I doing here?" and don't get stuck on one answer.

Child's Question: How do you take care of your sadness and anger?

Cheri Maples: When I'm sad, I like to lie on the ground and look at the sky and look at the clouds. I know that I'm really the big sky and my sadness is like the clouds; it will move away. I also like to be with animals. I like to go and pet my dog, because it makes me happy right away. I like to remember that I wouldn't know what happiness is if I didn't know what sadness was. The other thing I am always learning is to take a breath so that I don't speak when I'm angry. I can wait.

Child's Question: How do you deal with someone who died before you were born, and not knowing really how to miss them?

Sister Chau Nghiem: The feeling of missing someone can be a nice feeling. If someone has died before we were born and we didn't get to know them, we can still feel connected to them. We can even miss them. Maybe people share with us what they knew about that person and pass on what they loved about that person to us. Then we have the same memories, we can picture that person, and we love them through the love our mother and our father or other family members have for that person.

My mother's father died when she was very young; she was only six. I've only seen a picture of my grandfather, and he is smiling a beautiful smile. When I see that smile, I think of my brother. My brother has the same smile as our grandfather. People don't talk too much about him; he died when he was very young. But once when I was in Vietnam, we monks and nuns were doing a big ceremony of healing for the many people who suffered from the war in Vietnam. We were chanting all night long, we didn't eat, we didn't get up to go to the bathroom; we stayed chanting all night long. Thousands and thousands of people were chanting together and praying together. I was praying for all of my ancestors, and for all of my ancestors in this country—not just in my blood family, but for my Native American ancestors who suffered a lot, for the people who suffered in slavery, for those who died in the Civil War. Then I began to focus on my blood ancestors and I felt a very deep feeling of connectedness to my grandfather who I never met. We were walking together, holding hands. I felt so much love and true connectedness, and in that moment I knew that he didn't die; he was alive in my mother, because without him my mother couldn't be alive. He was alive in me, because without him my mother couldn't have made me with my father. So I think we can miss the people we love that we haven't met yet, and we can touch their presence still there in us.

If the person whom we're missing had some pain, some suffering, we can also help them to heal that in our own life through our own peaceful practice of breathing and walking. If we feel we missed something because we didn't get to meet that person, we can talk to them about that. We can make a vase of flowers and offer it as a gift to that person, because that person's always there in us.

Question: I recently had a conversation with a woman police officer who spoke about her frustration with being unable to change the culture at her work. There was a culture of not speaking the truth about things that felt uncomfortable. There was an in-group and an out-group. I know that probably many of us work in organizations that have a system that's very top-down. How can we mindfully help with systems change?

Cheri Maples: I can remember, as a young activist, doing everything from a place of great energy and self-righteousness: "The system was bad." And then I ended up in the system. Usually what I have found in changing an organizational culture is that the first and most important thing is to understand that change doesn't have to come from top-down. Just because the boss doesn't do it doesn't mean that I shouldn't do it.

What I have found to be the most stressful thing in any organization, whether it's a nonprofit, a paramilitary organization, a collective—and by the way I didn't find working in a feminist collective any easier than in a paramilitary organization—is the complex power dynamics at work. Sometimes when the power structure is more informal and hidden, it can be harder.

With the police officers I've worked with, I started to notice that we were teaching them how to keep themselves safe physically and about the technical parts of the job, but we weren't teaching them how to keep themselves safe emotionally. There were unspoken and unconscious agreements in the organization and a lot of gossip, which I think is the most stressful thing in any organization. I really try hard not to make people the enemy.

I found that I could really make a difference by not saying, "I'm the boss and you're going to do this," but by getting people together and saying, "How do we want to communicate with each other?" I also need to say, "Let's set some ground rules. But let's not set anything that we are not willing to do and call each other on."

When I was captain of personnel and training in the police department, I brought the Fourth Mindfulness Training to my team and I said, "What would it feel like to work on a team where there isn't gossip, where if you have a complaint you take it directly to the person, rather than to somebody else. What do you think? Do you want to have that as a ground rule?" They did. Then, as they were teaching the recruits, it became part of the recruit culture, too, and all these little factions started disappearing.

The other example I can give you is, there was an unspoken agreement and we were socialized that, as cops, certain things happen: you don't get a ticket from another cop, you get a free cup of coffee in a cafe, or you go hang out in a certain place. It was never talked about. It's just like some of our other unearned assets—privileges we may have because we're white, because we're heterosexual, because we're male—that are never talked about. The way that you change ethics in an organization is that you bring those unconscious and unspoken agreements into the conscious arena for discussion. You model that what you stand for personally is important because inner integrity is infinite. You can do it, as long as you check your intention.

Question: In my daily life, sometimes I think I'm just being a good actress, acting peaceful and looking like I should be part of this organization. But internally it's just turmoil and negativity, so I'm kind of scared to keep meditating. One night, I dreamed all about anger, the next night about jealousy, the next night about fear, and the next night about lying and cheating. I'm feeling a little shell-shocked.

Sister Huong Nghiem: Many friends experience this, particularly in a long retreat. As we settle and we look deep within, when we allow our mind to be still, then things that we have within us are there for us to be able to recognize. All of us have all the different types of seeds within our consciousness. It's important just to be able to acknowledge the presence of these seeds, just to know that they're there and know what may trigger them to come up. We can see them as our best friend, as our little girl or little boy within, and take their hand and be with them.

It could be that in the past, in the years before you had the practice, you didn't have a tool to take care of them, so we sort of shove them away and store them in our basement. Now we're allowing them a chance to be recognized. So we're just there for them. Take the walks you need to take. And assess how strong you are at the time. If you're not strong yet, then do things that would strengthen your foundation of joy, clarity, and stability. You might want to voice to your friends and family members that you're seeing things that are difficult for you to deal with, so they know and won't add more to your plate. Take care of it one bit at a time, and go deeper and deeper. I sense from my experience that all the different things may come from one root. They're just using different ways of trying to catch your attention. You're not giving them the attention they need. So they're masquerading as different characters to catch your attention.

Don't be fearful, because this is part of you. Meditation isn't to divide ourselves into a battlefield. Our anger and our sadness are part of us. If we don't take care of them no one else can help us. They can point something out for us, but we need to be able to recognize it and accept it. Accepting it doesn't mean we leave it like that. Accepting it means allowing it to be as it is for the time being, until we have the strength and the clarity to better take care of it, heal it, and transform it.

Question: My question is about the importance of both the individual practice that we do on our own, as well as the practice that we're supposed to do in the larger community, sort of reaching out to others. It's a little easier for me to be introspective, so I'm also looking for advice on how to bring my practice out to other people, to reach other people.

Sister Huong Nghiem: There's a gentleman who sometimes comes to Deer Park for our family retreat. I don't know what particular work he does, but something to do with websites, and he's in this Silicon Valley type of company. He says he just schedules a meeting room for a certain hour of the day for sitting meditation and he puts out on a bulletin that anyone who wants to come and sit with him is welcome. There's no structure to it, just a chance to be quiet and sit quietly. He said there would be days when there were ten people, days when there were five, and there were three or four who came routinely and they started getting to know each other. So the people don't need to be from the same tradition. It's just to be able to have a space where you can have meditation for the time you can allot to it in your busy life.

Question: My question is about Beginning Anew with someone with whom you have a violent history. I grew up in an abusive, violent family. My father was very abusive toward my mother and my sisters and me. I am still dealing with a lot of anger and sadness from that time. Now my father is eighty-seven, he's had a series of health problems and strokes, so my husband and I had to step in and provide care for him. That's caused me to have a lot of resentment because now I feel I'm forced into the situation. I need to make things right for myself, for my family, for my children.

Brother Phap Tri: It's difficult to Begin Anew with someone who doesn't want to practice or know about the practice, because then the Beginning Anew relies on you. You have to practice for them, even though they might not realize that you're practicing for them. To do that can be a little bit challenging. So we have to look at the historic nature of our relationship, to look at ways in which we can transform our part in the relationship.

   I know with my own mother, before I became a practitioner, I wanted her to be different. She was about seventy years old and she wasn't going to really become somebody else just for me. As I continued to practice, I understood more and more how I needed to not only love my mother unconditionally, but to find a way in myself to accept her love unconditionally, in whatever way that may have manifested, however she was able to offer it. This helped me tremendously in transforming my relationship with her.

I also realized when we have a difficult relationship, especially with a parent, we have to look within ourselves, to look at our relationship with our parent, and to look at our parent to see more deeply into why they are the way they are. This is the basis of the guided meditation on the five-year-old child. Because our parents were also once a little five-year-old child, very vulnerable, like we were when they might have abused us. At one time in their life, they were also that vulnerable child. They may just be repeating a cycle that was transmitted to them by their parents. Usually when a person is abusive or violent with us, whether a family member or another person, it's a manifestation of the suffering that is within that person. So we need to look at ways in which we can be safe and not be abused by that person but also be okay with that person, instead of reacting to them and watering the seed of our negative history with them. This may be very difficult to do because, depending on the nature of the abuse, it can be very internalized. It's in every cell of our body. If we've been carrying it around for forty years or more, that way of thinking is very ingrained in our mind and our heart and our body.

We want to find a way of responding to this situation, to this father, because he's not going to change. The more we push against him, the more he experiences negative reinforcement. But if, instead, we can find a way to be soft with him, to be loving and gentle, then by transforming our part in the relationship, we have Begun Anew with our father. In some ways it's a very complex practice, but in some ways it's not. We just have to really be patient with ourselves and get a lot of community support. It's very helpful if we can have the support of our family, our partner, our friends.

Of course your father is elderly, and we don't know if you're going to be able to heal your relationship with him before he passes from this life. Many times when people begin to pass from this life, they start to transform some of their habit energies in a very beautiful way that actually opens the door for transformation and healing in their primary relationships, with their family members. If he already feels this on a very subtle level, and if he can be surrounded by the people he has had a historically violent relationship with, it can open the door for this to happen.

Question: I heard the term "radical intimacy" the other day and I've seen a lot of loving families here that are very tactile and close to each other. I've been a single father for eight years and I've raised adolescents into early adulthood. I think I'm a good father, but I am a male and was brought up in the John Wayne era, and I find it hard to express the kind of intimacy that I see and that I think is really necessary to the practice.

I phoned my two daughters on their cell phones and they weren't in and at the end of it I, gulp, said: "love you," but it was kind of perfunctory. I also come from an ethnic group that doesn't have a lot of warmth. My son and I have about a five-second male hug. I don't know how it is for other people, but it's a really big barrier for me. I'd like some insight on that.

Cheri Maples: We often think insight is always the first step in the practice, but sometimes you have to act your way into a new way of thinking. Action is sometimes just as simple as: "My intention is to soften. My intention in this moment is to soften and open my heart, and to start over and over and over." Each moment of warmth, of physical expression, accumulates.

Rowan Conrad: You want to be able to express your deep connection to your children. It would be very valuable to just tell your children this. We spend a lot of time hiding, but what is there to hide? Let them know what you feel and ask them if more expression is something they would want. Ask them, "Is this something you want? Is this something we can find a way to address?"

Question: Thay says that we have to give up all notions. In some forms of Buddhism we do that, I think, by meditating and attaining certain states of consciousness or concentration, or practicing koans and developing some state of mind that allows us to give up all our notions. I guess my question is, in this tradition how do we give up all our notions?

Sister Huong Nghiem: How do you explain love to your child? By the way you express it, the way you embody it, the way you share it with your child, she learns love, she knows love, but she doesn't need to have a notion of love.

During the 2007 North America tour when Thay introduced the meditation on letting the Buddha sit or walk for us, it was very difficult for many people to see that and to be able to see and touch the Buddha within themselves. But already, from what I hear, many people at this retreat have expressed that because Thay's physical presence is not here, everyone is sitting straighter, everyone is actually practicing, deepening their own practice. So the concentration of impermanence becomes a practice, it's no longer a notion. We are actually touching and tasting the impermanence, and we're actually living it and using it and not being fearful of it; we're actually being able to see Thay in each one of us. Many people have mentioned that they not only see Thay within the long-term practitioners, but also in every single person, even if it's that person's first retreat—they can see the intention of that person to practice. So it's no longer something in the intellect, but people are really feeling it and seeing it as an energy and working with it.

So already I see in our retreat Sangha that it's no longer a notion. It's not something we have in our mind but really feel in our heart. One woman said that she has never seen Thay and she wanted to see him at this retreat, but somehow she feels like she knows Thay and actually cares for him even though she hasn't been able to see him. She's read Thay's books and has been able to practice Thay's teachings in a way that have made a difference her life. So somehow we truly integrate the practice in our life. It's not like putting on a shirt and taking it off. It's actually a change of lifestyle, a way of looking at things.

S H A R I N G S

Cathy Bradshaw

It was Sunday morning, two days before the retreat was to end. I had been amazed at the peace, insight, gentleness, kindness, and calm of the two previous days. I was feeling that I had finally tapped into the present moment as I have never done in my life. I felt surrounded by the beauty of the environment and a warm closeness to the Sangha.

I awoke around 5:00 A.M. in a panic. I felt so sad and anxious about having to return home and face my busy work life, my kids' school and life challenges, a boyfriend who I had recently ended a relationship with. The feelings were very intense. I could say it bordered on a panic attack. My heart was beating so fast and I felt paralyzed. Then I remembered that these were seeds of sadness and fear that had come up from my store consciousness. I recognized them and then remembered that I also had seeds of compassion and understanding in my store consciousness that I could call up to help deal with these other seeds.

My compassion and understanding spoke to my sadness and fear. They said, "I can understand how sad you must be to think about leaving this beautiful place and all the peaceful experiences you have had here. Anyone would feel sad saying goodbye to this beauty." They said, "Please know that we are here for you and that we will help you to bring all this beauty back home with you to help deal with your life. You are not alone. We will take good care of you."

I doubt I can capture how wonderful this experience was, but my fear and sadness faded rather quickly. My fear and sadness somehow felt like they had been honored and loved. I've spent most of my life either chastising my feelings or running away from them. It amazed me how gracefully they left once they were acknowledged, respected, and cared for.

Instead of Words by Esther Kamkar

Instead of words
Black on white
Strung on a wire
Formed into hooks
To hang our longings
We need warm skins
Eyes, hands
And lips to say:
This is it and
It is enough
We need
Listening hearts
Pumping:
Yes, I
Hear you
Hear you
Hear you.

Sister Hanh Nghiem

In Colorado, I was in charge of about sixteen teens. They were such a mixture of personalities, yet they managed to stick together and support each other to practice. One girl said, "I cannot believe how well we get along and manage to hang out together, although we are so different." On the day of the Be-in, the "talent" show, we didn't have anything to offer. We thought we could come up with something on the hike.When we sat for lunch, we had a lot of fun brainstorming. Someone suggested we do the song "Come Together" by the Beatles. We ended there, saying we would meet up at 6 P.M. after we got back, to see what we could do with this song once we had the lyrics and the guitar chords.

I really had little hope that this would all pull together. We were all a bit tired and we all needed some freshening up. It was already 5 P.M. Instead of hurrying off to our rooms we were stopped by some deer. We sat there at the side of road, eating some chips and enjoying watching the deer nibbling away at the plant life. One of the teens offered out his hand for the deer to lick the salt off. The deer accepted the offering and the boy was blessed. Finally we all parted. With little faith I went to our cabin with the lyrics. Low and behold a couple of people were there and slowly they trickled into our meeting place. Two people were figuring out the chords on the piano, others were having a cushion fight, and a few of us were racking our brains to figure out the lyrics. Well we did it, just like the Beatles, we came together and it felt great.

Only the Essentials by Gratia Meyer

For the first time in forty-one years, I let go of one of my "cows," one of my attachments. I came to Colorado and I did not bring my original green mat and blue cushion, shawl, blue cloth bag with a journal, two pens, camera, nose spray, tissues, comb, lip balm, hand cream, knitted hat and gloves.

Instead, I sat comfortably on my brown cushion knowing that I could listen and no longer need to frantically write down every minute detail of the Dharma. I was comfortable being in the present moment.

When I learned that Thay was not going to join us—in corporal form—at the 2009 Estes Park Retreat, I sat and reflected on how we had gotten to this moment. I was in the hospital in 1968 when I first read Thay's book *The Cry of Vietnam.* I was motivated to help Vietnamese orphans after reading his poem, "I Met You in the Orphanage Yard." Now many of the children of Vietnam that I worked with have grown up, are living in other countries, are married, and have children. In three weeks, I will meet my future daughter-in-law who is coming from Thai Binh Province.

While I meditated on Vulture Peak recently, I received a riddle: If you remove the *t* from "not thinking," you have "no thinking." In Vietnamese, *t* translates as "tan," which means change. By removing *t*, we remove our notions of nonbeing, nondiscrimination, nonjudgment, and non-grasping. How freeing to let go of my attachments to the practice! Over the years, I have strategically placed my cushion in the front row of the Sangha, carried my "essential belongings," and followed Thay to Vietnam, India, the U.S., and Plum Village, France. On the last day of the Colorado retreat, I became aware that I really didn't need any of these things. Thay has been within me all of the time. I need only to just stop and practice.

Nine Hundred Buddhas Is a Good Start
by Maureen Lancaster

Fall is here now. I watch the blowing leaves and the snow out my window. The retreat in Estes Park is still very much alive in my heart.

I remember taking a walk when I heard you were ill, dear Thay. My fear and sadness walked with me. Then I felt your unconditional love and warm compassion enfold me and infuse every cell in my body. You weren't there physically, but in that moment, I was holding your hand and walking with you. I made a promise in that moment to take that compassion out into the world with me every day.

After that, I saw the Buddha in every person there, the very small Buddhas and the not-so-young part-time Buddhas. You were there in each person's eyes and heart and feet and breath. I still see and hear all the wonderful nuns and monks and their incredible courage and compassion as they stepped in and offered us their experience of the Dharma, their experience of you, dear Thay. The gifts they gave us in their teachings are very, very precious, and you were there in each one.

You were everywhere that week! The Buddha, the Dharma and the Sangha filled the Rocky Mountains! I can still hear Brother Wayne describe holding your hand as a young monk, swinging your arms together, and you asked, "Are you ready to go to the Pure Land? One…two…three…let's go!"

The Sangha answered "Yes, let's go!" just as Brother Wayne did. The Sangha river went forth from Estes Park carrying the Dharma and filling the mountains with the sounds of joy. The river is still going, carried by the feet of the 900 people there.

Whose Breath? by Michelle Zande

The earth holds us
like curious treasures
in its open palm.
Fingertip mountains cradle
our hush, our reverence.

The sky peers sleepily
over a blanket of softly folded clouds
gazing down with pillow-pinked cheek.
Underneath, black birds trace
joyous pathways across the sky.

Dry grasses bend, lay, spring back
bowing, touching the earth.
We walk our quiet pathway.
The earth lets out a sigh and
the aspen starts to sing.

you
continue
in
us

10: You Continue In Us: A Hospital Diary

Brother Phap Nguyen (Dharma Aspiration)

AUGUST 13, 2009

A NUMBER OF us monks and nuns took Thay to the hospital to have his lungs examined. In the beginning, I thought this would be a routine medical examination at a facility specializing in pulmonary diseases. I did not realize it would be such a large hospital. Getting out of the van, I could feel the hurried and heavy hospital atmosphere. We followed Thay in his walk to the hospital entrance—Thay practiced walking meditation, as he does wherever he goes.

While waiting for the doctor, I served Thay some hot tea and then went outside to let Brother Phap Huy know that it could be a long wait. Brother Phap Huy replied calmly, "No problem. I'll just sit and breathe!"

The doctor arrived. A large, bespectacled man, he introduced himself as Dr. Sicilian and shook Thay's hand. He asked, "The patient I was referred to is 'Thich Nhat Hanh,' but the name on the paperwork is 'Thay.' Which is the right name?" We explained that friends and students of Thich Nhat Hanh call him "Thay," which means teacher. Dr. Sicilian asked how he should address Thay. Thay smiled and said, "You can call me Thay as well."

Dr. Sicilian then showed us the CT scan images. Bacteria had infected many areas in Thay's lungs, which appeared white instead of

the healthy black color. The doctor said that new tests showed that Thay needed to stop everything and get treated immediately.

Thay, who knew his condition better than anyone, decided after some deliberation to continue leading the Massachusetts retreat. After the retreat ended, depending on the results from the phlegm and blood work, he would decide whether or not to be hospitalized.

AUGUST 17, 2009

The Stonehill retreat was completed successfully yesterday. This morning, the monastic Sangha headed for Denver, Colorado, to prepare for the next retreat at the Estes Park YMCA. There was a joyful atmosphere at our dormitories as the brothers and sisters were preparing for the trip. There were sounds of suitcase locks clicking here and there. Outside, a few birds were hopping around, greeting a new day. It was dawn.

Thay woke up at 5:25 A.M. He enjoyed the cup of tea the way the birds outside welcome a new day—in peace and freedom. Finished with the tea, Thay stood up and put on his robe. Knowing his desire

to go out, I helped him with his coat, and we went outside for walking meditation. It was past 6:00 A.M. and the sun was already up. We did walking meditation outside the dormitories. With each step we were aware that this was our last morning here at Stonehill. We wanted to fully enjoy the peace and beauty of this place. In a parking lot, Thay pointed to a bumper sticker that said, "My other vehicle is the Mahayana." We smiled and continued our walk.

At 6:00 P.M., we accompanied Thay to the hospital. After we identified ourselves, the door opened and a nurse named Heather came out, gave us each a mask to wear, and led us to Thay's room. In order to enter the room, one had to go through two doors; the first door had to be closed before the second could be opened. Seeing this operation, Brother Phap Huy exclaimed, "We're used to this!" Brother Phap Huy was right. Going through two doors in this way is how we go through at Thay's huts in order to keep out the wind. Here, the two-door design was to prevent any dangerous microorganism from escaping to the outside. The hospital was very thorough in its precautionary practice. Between the two doors were a sink and a table for medical supplies. In the room were a table, two nightstands, a study desk, two chairs, a small round table for food, a wall TV, and toilet facilities. The room was small but comfortable. A beautiful view of Boston could be seen through the large glass window.

AUGUST 18, 2009

We got up at dawn. I served Thay a cup of hot tea while we waited for Brother Phap Huy and the sisters. Through the glass window, Boston looked beautiful in the morning. When the sisters came with food, we laid out breakfast in the small area on the floor next to Thay's bed. This area was becoming a multipurpose venue: it was a dining area, sleeping quarters, and perhaps this afternoon or tomorrow it would be Thay's calligraphy studio. The eight of us had a happy breakfast together. We did not have the feeling of being in a hospital; on this first day, the place already felt like home to us.

At 12:15 P.M. Dr. Sicilian arrived. He informed us that the analysis of the sputum showed 95% likelihood that the bacterium in the sputum was not tuberculosis (TB), which left 5% likelihood that it was TB. This was because they had found a type of bacterium, as yet to be identified, which they temporarily called mycobacteria. They thought this bacterium could be a variant of TB bacterium. It could be harmful or harmless, but since it was new to them, the lab needed more time to analyze more phlegm. We had some doubt about the TB diagnosis but it was too early to comment.

Thay said, "You should check again. Maybe the bacterium came from the environment." Thay meant that the bacterium could have come from the atmosphere or contaminated hospital utensils. The doctor said that it could be so, but very unlikely. We knew the picture would become clearer in a few days, so we refrained from making any other comments.

AUGUST 19, 2009

Betty, the attending nurse, came in at 6:30 A.M. to measure Thay's vital signs and administer the antibiotics. Thay had not yet shown any response to the treatment. His cough still contained phlegm and sometimes a little blood. Since the blood analysis showed high levels of enzymes in Thay's liver and spleen, the doctor had planned for Thay to undergo ultrasound examination of his internal organs.

At 10:00 A.M., a hospital staff person brought a gurney to bring Thay to ultrasound, but Nurse Theresa said, "It's okay, I'll walk him down." She sent the gurney away and telephoned the ultrasound section to let them know she would walk there with Thay and would take responsibility for any mishap. I followed Thay in walking meditation to the ultrasound area downstairs. Theresa was observing with interest that Thay was walking with peace and serenity. At ultrasound, we were asked to sit and wait for the examination, and to telephone Theresa when done.

Sitting down on the bench, Thay said, "My child, this also is a revolution." He was referring to the idea that, like in Buddhism, the hospital had its many regulations—hospital gown, mask, transportation by gurney, etc. Yet they had been willing to let Thay wear his own monastic robe and walk here. They had shown a revolutionary spirit.

It was nearly noon when we returned to Thay's room to have our brunch. It appeared we always had a party in the room, with a lot of happy laughter. The sisters had purchased a broom, dustpan, and dishwashing detergent for the room. Brother Phap Don felt embarrassed for bringing a broom and dustpan into the hospital. Who in the world would bring things like that into a hospital? But we had turned this hospital room into our home. We felt very happy and spacious being near Thay each day here. We swept and mopped the floor, washed the dishes, and tidied up the room. The custodians loved us because we did all the work for them. They only needed to provide a few trash bags.

At around 3 P.M., Dr. Sicilian came with another physician. All the ultrasound results were good. The lab still could not determine the nature of the mycobacteria. Despite the fact that the bacteria were found only with the first of the four phlegm samples, the hospital still

suspected TB and wanted to treat Thay for it. Thay had a long discussion with the doctors and rejected the proposed TB treatment.

Thay observed that since the lab could not identify the mycobacteria, the doctors, based on other assessments, had assigned a probability (of 5%) to the bacteria being TB—but now this assessment had become a concept that the doctors felt was impossible to discard. Thay said that in Buddhism, it was necessary to abandon all concepts in order to acquire the right view of reality. It appeared the doctors had hypothesized that Thay's illness was due to one of three cases: (1) Thay had only the bacteria Pseudomonas aeruginosa, (2) Thay had only TB bacteria, or (3) Thay had both types of bacteria.

Thay said to Dr. Sicilian, "But to me, those three scenarios are still not sufficient. We should have a fourth scenario, which is that Thay has neither type of bacteria."

Sister Chan Khong gave the example of a friend who was wrongly diagnosed with TB and was treated with TB drugs for his pulmonary symptoms. It was only after the powerful medicines had killed him that it was discovered that he did not have TB.

Thay suggested a similarity in the way the Iraq war had started, based on a belief that Iraq possessed weapons of mass destruction.

The country was destroyed and none of these weapons were found. He said the human body is not a battlefield; one should not provide a course of treatment without clear knowledge of the illness.

The two doctors listened attentively to Thay and Sister Chan Khong. I empathized with both sides. It appeared that Dr. Sicilian could appreciate Thay's view, but he still had considerable suspicion that Thay had TB. He said that at the moment, Thay should not use public transportation. This posed a potentially great threat to the rest of the tour, which would cover Colorado, Mississippi, California, and New York.

At our request, the hospital agreed not to measure Thay's vital signs in the evening, and allowed Thay to go outside for walking meditation this afternoon with the condition that he had to wear a face mask. This was just as Thay had observed: the hospital had its rules, but they also made exceptions to these rules, which was revolutionary.

At 4:45 P.M., we went out to the river for walking meditation. It was warm but rather windy. At the end of the walk, we sat down on the riverbank watching the little boats going to and fro in the river. I offered Thay a cup of hot tea. After three days in the hospital, this was the first time we had been able to enjoy the fresh air outside. Thay was delighted.

AUGUST 20, 2009

To open my eyes in the morning and see Thay still here for us was a moment of happiness. Having been in the hospital now for a few days, I've had the opportunity to observe and contemplate impermanence more concretely. Everything is impermanent, including Thay's physical form. I've treasured every moment that Thay is here with us.

I had a wonderful moment with Thay recently at Stonehill College. One day, Thay wanted to visit the cafeteria and have breakfast with the community. Halfway through our walking meditation to the cafeteria, he turned to me, "My child, do you know that you are very lucky? Otherwise, I could be gone like your Uncle Teacher." Thay was referring to his junior lineage brother who had passed away two weeks before. I nodded and replied quietly, "Yes." But in my heart, my answer was actually very loud, "Dear Thay, I always treasure every minute of your presence."

After breakfast, we took a walk on the riverbank. The temperature outside was very comfortable. We did walking meditation along the beautiful path. On the way back, we ran into a Vietnam veteran who immediately recognized Thay. He came in front of Thay, joined his palms and bowed. Thay returned the bow.

The man said, "Are you Thich Nhat Hanh? You are a good man. I read all of your books. I was in Vietnam, but I didn't kill anyone." He appeared happy and surprised to meet Thay. Thay held his hand, and they smiled to each other. Thay appreciated the man's remark. On the way back to the hospital, he smiled and repeated the sentence, "I was in Vietnam, but I didn't kill anyone." Thay's smile radiated much inner peace.

While drinking tea back in his room, Thay shared his insight on the interbeing nature of war and peace. There is peace because there is war. Peace exists inside war. It was due to the war that Thay ended up living in and sharing Buddhism with the West. Thanks to the war, Plum Village and many other mindfulness practice centers came into existence, bringing much peace and calm to people all over the world.

Thay asked when he could begin doing calligraphy. I replied that we were ready to set it up whenever Thay felt inclined to start. Thay wanted to begin right away, and the room immediately became a calligraphy studio. Thay wrote many calligraphies, including quite a few circles.

Later in the morning, a group of doctors from the Department of Infectious Diseases came for a visit. Among them was a Dr. Stamm, who had maintained a strong suspicion that Thay had TB. The doctors shared what information they'd been able to find so far, which was nothing new to us.

I asked, "All tests after the first one have shown no sign of tuberculosis or mycobacteria. Even if all future analyses of additional specimens are negative, are you still thinking Thay might have tuberculosis?"

Dr. Stamm replied, "That's right."

Thay said, "In Buddhism, this is called clinging to views."

Thay repeated his earlier suggestion, "Maybe the bacteria came from the environment, not from me."

Dr. Stamm replied, "It's possible, but it's highly unlikely."

Thay said, "If we are not sure that the bacteria are TB, we should not administer anti-TB drugs to the body. To do so would turn the body into a battlefield when we do not know for sure whether an enemy exists. We should be open-minded to the possibility I have neither tuberculosis or mycobacteria."

Dr. Stamm replied, "Yes, I agree. We should be open-minded. It's not only true in the medical field, but it's true also in everything in life." The doctors appeared to be yielding to this logic.

Later, Dr. Sicilian came and appeared to have seriously considered Thay's comments. He said the lab was making a large culture of the mycobacteria found in the first sample. The larger size of the culture would facilitate further analyses.

AUGUST 21, 2009

Last night we were woken up twice by medical technicians coming in to check Thay's vital signs despite our earlier request that no such work be done in the evening. Then it happened again at 12:30 A.M., after which the technician was able to put a stop to the practice by posting a sign outside the door to communicate the request to the next shift.

Thay woke up at around 6:00 A.M. It was a beautiful morning. Outside, the scenery was very peaceful and we, too, felt much at peace. I related the story of the disturbances of last night to the sisters who had come with breakfast, and we composed a humorous poem on the subject:

> *Don't check vital signs*
> *I'm still alive*
> *Please be kind*
> *Stay behind*

After breakfast, we practiced walking meditation toward the river. The sun was shining and there was a light breeze. In front of us was a park with large, shady trees. Thay sat resting on a bench, enjoying the cup of hot tea that I'd offered and contemplating the river. Suddenly, Thay gave a slight cough. There was only a little blood in the phlegm! Thay looked tired and lay down on the small blanket I'd rolled up for him as a pillow. After some time, Brother Phap Huy brought pen and paper, and Thay sat up to write a letter to the participants of the Colorado retreat. It was likely that at this point, no one in the retreat knew yet that Thay would not be present. Our concern was that Thay's absence would greatly disappoint the retreatants.

I immediately faxed the letter to Colorado so it could be read to the

retreatants in the evening. I hoped that our lay brothers and sisters in the retreat would be able to feel Thay's love through this letter.

Of these happenings, Thay simply said, "Everything must have been arranged by our spiritual ancestors." I was moved to recall the story in the Lotus Sutra about a physician who decided to go away from home when his sick children refused to take the medicine that would cure them. A while later, the physician sent news that he had died so that his children could no longer depend on having a good father for a doctor. As a result of the father's action, the children began to take the medicines and they were cured. The situation seemed similar here, except Thay was not pretending to be ill. This could be an opportunity for retreatants to learn to practice without Thay's physical form. This would also be an opportunity for us monastics to actualize ourselves and prove that we were indeed Thay's continuation.

In bed, Thay told a story about a time when the Chinese king named Thanh Vuong went hunting. His servants had wanted to use a net to completely surround the forest in which the king would hunt. The king told his subjects not to set up the net to completely surround the animals but to allow them an opening—whichever animals could escape, allow them to escape.

The teaching in the story was that we should never force a person or animal into a desperate situation, as this would cause the subject to react very strongly and out of desperation, with unpredictable results. Thay related this to his reasoning on why he shouldn't take drugs for a disease that he probably didn't have. Thay often reminds us that the seed of compassion exists in everyone, and he could see the seed of compassion in the doctor through the doctor's reasoning.

Later, Thay had physical therapy. At the therapist's request, Thay showed her his breathing method to expel his sputum. She was deeply impressed and said, "Wow, you're a professional breather!"

AUGUST 22, 2009

This morning, Thay said it would be great to have a hammock near the river. Fortunately, we had brought a hammock with us, and we set it up between two tree branches on the riverbank. Thay was delighted to be enjoying the hammock and the cup of tea we offered. Perhaps this was the first time ever that a patient was allowed to come and go freely from the hospital, even to enjoy a hammock near the river. The air was fresh and the weather comfortable. In the water I could see a long neck crane walking about looking for food. The scenery was lovely, and I could see that Thay was very happy. And I felt happy, seeing that Thay was happy. Just like Thay has taught, "Happiness is not an individual matter."

After dinner, we telephoned Colorado to get the latest news. Sister Thoai Nghiem related that during Dharma discussion today, many people shared that they were trying to learn to recognize Thay's presence in themselves. Most people came for the opportunity to see, listen to, and benefit from Thay's personal instructions. Still, many first-time retreatants were able to enjoy the retreat without Thay. This was above and beyond anything we had imagined.

We were very happy with this news. We could see a clear indication of the successful continuation of Thay. I think Thay was very happy and reassured by this concrete sign of his continuation. He said, "Perhaps all this has been arranged by our spiritual ancestors, and this is the test."

AUGUST 23, 2009

This noon, we talked with Sister Hy Nghiem at the Colorado retreat. She informed us that the retreatants were carrying on very well. She related many interesting and beautiful stories about the retreat. Thay was deeply happy. Thay suggested that we ask whether the retreatants would be willing to come back each year for a retreat led by Plum Village monastics, and not wait to have a retreat led by Thay only every other year. To Thay, this was an opportunity for the Sangha to practice without Thay. He had seen the maturity of the monastic Sangha and its ability to be his continuation.

AUGUST 24, 2009

Thay had been at the hospital for eight days, yet it seemed like he'd been admitted only yesterday. We had created much joy and happiness for ourselves here because we were able to accept this place as home. There were many unexpected events. Thay had to stay longer in the hospital and, therefore, he could not lead the Colorado retreat. Initially, we did not know how retreatants would react. There were concerns about the retreat, the retreatants, and Thay's health during the first few days, especially before Thay's hospital admission. But looking back now, it seemed everything worked out favorably, just as Thay had predicted.

Without Thay at the retreat, the brothers and sisters had to work together more closely and diligently. The retreatants also practiced more diligently in Thay's absence.

AUGUST 25, 2009

Dr. Sicilian came in early this morning. We were surprised to see him without a mask. He made an important declaration: Thay did not have TB. The doctor also said that Thay's blood counts had increased. This was good news because the high blood counts would help Thay's immune system fight off any invading bacteria.

So today was Thay's last day in the hospital. While having breakfast together in this cozy room, the fourteen of us were keenly aware that this would be our last breakfast here. Thay told the story of Vimalakirti who, while ill, was visited in his small room by the Bodhisattva Manjushri and others. There were so many visitors, yet the small room was able to contain them all. This hospital room of Thay has also been like that. Normally it would be crowded with just a few people, and here we were, all fourteen together at the same time.

Lunch today consisted of bread and boxed vegetarian dishes. With everything loaded into the cars, I had only to bring a hammock and tea to the picnic area. We sat on paper bags, and Thay on a rock covered with cloth towels. The lunch was simple and light, and we felt close to Thay in this simplicity.

Reflecting on what we have been through the last nine days at the hospital with Thay, it has been a once in a lifetime experience for all of us. It's amazing to see how many lives Thay has touched, even while he was hospitalized. During the hospital stay, Thay used his time very effectively and efficiently. So much love and compassion could be seen from his actions. His insight was constantly flowing, like a waterfall. The Dharma was present everywhere Thay went, not only in Thay's speech but also silently through his thoughts and actions.

Thay was very solid in every way—dwelling in the present moment and strongly capable of living joyfully, peacefully, and happily in the here and now. This was very clear during Thay's nine-day hospital stay. And, being a part of this experience, one could directly see and learn the benefit of living and viewing life from the optimistic view rather than the pessimistic view. The key to it, as Thay has taught us, is to live mindfully in every moment of our lives, dwelling peacefully in the here and the now.

Love Letter Two

August 24, 2009

Dear Friends,

This is Thay again writing to you from the Massachusetts General Hospital. The treatment is going well. Thank you for having sent your loving energy. I learned that you all, both monastic and lay members of the Sangha, have practiced beautifully with all your hearts in the retreat. That makes me very happy. The most wonderful thing is that after a few moments of sadness, worry, and disappointment, all of us have settled down to practice and conduct the retreat the most wonderful way a Sangha could. The transformation and the joy you feel presently at the retreat is very nourishing and encouraging for me and for every one of us. By now all of us have already seen the talent and the miracle of the Sangha. We have to acknowledge the fact that the Sangha has embodied the continuation of the Buddha in a beautiful way, and there is no reason for any one of us to worry about the future of our practice. King Prasenajit of Shravasti one day told the Buddha that when he observed the Sangha, he could truly see the Buddha. One of the achievements of this retreat is that everyone can see Thay in the Sangha, including those who come to the retreat for the first time.

The Sangha is quite capable to continue the work of the Buddha and of our ancestral teachers. I would like to propose that the Colorado

Retreat become an annual retreat in the tradition of Plum Village; and that all of you, as conditions permitted, will come together as members of the Sangha to allow other people to have a chance to practice the Dharma. Thus every one of us in this retreat becomes a continuation of the teachings. Much happiness has come to my heart every time I remember that I have already had a beautiful continuation. I have full confidence in the Sangha, and trust that my Sangha will always be able to perform the miracle of the practice, whether with or without my physical presence.

Thank you again all my friends and students, and I hope to see you again very soon.

Love and trust,
Thay

S H A R I N G S

Cheri Maples

What was special for me was to observe people practicing and the wonderful practice container that was created by everybody present. Sometimes I notice that when Thay is doing walking meditation, there are lines of people ahead of him trying to take his picture rather than doing walking meditation. Of course, this did not happen at this retreat. People were practitioners rather than observers of Thay. I think he would like that. I'm left with a feeling of pride, confidence, and overwhelming love for the entire Sangha, especially the monastics who demonstrated the beauty of the practice in their Dharma talks, the sessions they led, and the way they conducted themselves and led the retreat. It was a model of loving leadership.

Karina Sabot

On the last day of the retreat, everything is packed into my truck. I walk around with a T-shirt embroidered in Tibetan symbols of blessings. I want to give it to someone as a gift. When I return to the hotel, the light on the hotel phone is blinking. The kennel says my dog, Tuzigoot, who was ill, has had a rough night. This means he died there. Now I know the Tibetan t-shirt will be his burial shroud.

A woman who cried in my arms at the retreat because a friend committed suicide holds me as I tell her about Tuzi-goot. "You are holding me as I cry today, as I held you crying when we arrived." We smile. We bow to the Buddhas within us.

Twenty-five Bunnies, Twenty-six Buddhas, and Eight Breaths
by Nancy Lee Koschmann

It's been almost a year since I flew to Colorado to attend the One Buddha Is Not Enough retreat with my Denver-based nieces, first grader Claire and third grader Audrey, and their mother, my sister Laurie. Thirty-three thousand feet above the earth and in the middle of the country, I was oblivious to the events taking place in Boston, where Thay was hospitalized for a serious lung infection. My thoughts were about morning meditations, sharing my nieces' first retreat experience, and Dharma discussions with my sister.

However, when one of the monastics announced that first night that she would read a letter from Thay, I knew exactly what it said. I had been at the Mindfulness Day in New York just a few weeks before, and I was not the only one there concerned about Thay's health. Thay had coughed often and his voice was even softer than usual. His message that day about the importance of Sangha as support for our practice and continuation of the teachings had a heartfelt ring to it.

I still remember my first reactions as the reading of the letter ended: sympathy for others' reactions, admittedly some regret that my nieces would not get to experience Thay in person, and powerful wishes for my teacher's health and well-being. If this had happened at my first retreat, I would have been both disappointed and a bit miffed; for many of us, it is no easy task to get together the money to travel, and I worried that others would have trouble reconciling their feelings. In my case, this Rockies retreat was, at the most fundamental level, an opportunity to practice taking refuge in the Sangha.

Claire and Audrey turned to us as they began to understand the letter. The many faces around us wore a plethora of expressions, but the girls were both frowning with concern. Their first questions were not about Thay's presence or absence, but about his health.

"Will Thay be okay?" Audrey wanted to know. "Is he very sick?"

Claire spoke softly, "He doesn't hurt, does he?"

Both were reassured when we pointed out that he'd said in the letter that he was allowed to walk in the park for an hour every day.

Claire was silent for a while and then said, "I wish I could walk with him and hold his hand so he knows we love him." Audrey was nodding as I met my sister's eyes: Claire had spoken for all of us.

Thay was very present at the retreat, not only for the adults—many of whom did struggle at first with disappointment, anger, or fear and concern about what this meant for their practice and the future of Thay's teachings—but also for the children, who put many of us to shame with their acceptance of the situation and their straightforward understanding that the teachings were what really mattered.

Every morning my four family members sat together on our cushions in the front of the auditorium. Audrey, being older and more sophisticated, listened carefully to the children's Dharma talks, punctuating her concentration with an occasional wave to one of her new friends or a whisper to her sister. Claire, however, hardly moved, sitting silently on her cushion with a far-away look in her eyes and my notebook and pen in her lap. From time to time, she scribbled something on a page. I assumed that because she was barely seven, much of the material was beyond her and she was entertaining herself by drawing pictures or practicing letters and numbers. Although both girls clearly loved the children's activities, my sister Laurie and I were not sure how much they were actually absorbing.

Because such retreats can sometimes feel like Buddhist boot camp to adult first timers and even more so to children, my sister suggested on the next-to-last morning that we give the children a short break from the constant activities. We would each take one of them for a little down time and special attention. When the children's Dharma talk was over, my sister took Audrey off for a walk in the woods while

Claire and I headed to our bunk beds to play. Not uncharacteristically, play for Claire was about her "work," which it turned out was what she had been doing with my notepad on her cushion.

Abandoned on the steps of an orphanage in China when she was just a few days old, Claire entered her new family at thirteen months, too small, too quiet, too fragile, too emotionally faraway.

Audrey had also come from China as a baby, but her outgoing nature gave her an advantage in adapting to a new situation. Like her older sister, Claire is always thinking, but unlike her sibling, she doesn't always share her thoughts. So I was deeply surprised and moved when Claire told me she wanted to copy over her poems so she could read to me what she had been writing every morning. She turned to the back pages of the notebook and began.

The first one, she explained, was a haiku:

25 BUNNIES

25 bunnies
26 boodas
8 breeths

"Bunnies are Buddhas too," she explained. "That's why we promise to protect them. And there are more than just one. All they have to do to be a Buddha is just breathe slowly, about eight times." I was feeling very foolish for having doubted what the girls were absorbing.

She quietly copied over two more poems and then read them to me.

How

How I walk
How the Booda metitates
How I breeth in and out
How I feel grass brushin
Along my legs
And the wind in my face
And the rain drops on my nose

is
Booda
Darma
Songa

BOODA

I see menny boodas
Around me,
Including the bell.
There is no booda in it?
You here the booda
With your ears.
Booda....

"Some Buddhas are invisible, " she said. "Like Thay here in the mountains." Of course. Silly me.

"And this is one of my songs I am going to play when I get home," she said, pointing at another page. Claire plays the violin, often just for fun and not because she should practice for her lessons. She had announced her desire to learn the violin two years earlier, and for her fifth birthday, my mother cajoled my sister into enrolling Claire in classes. Claire had wanted to bring her beloved instrument with her to the retreat, but my sister felt that even a very small violin was not going to be very welcome in the dormitory.

A Song

Breathe and you know that you are alive
Breathe and you know that all is helloing you
Breathe in your self, breath[e] in the world

"I want to write a song about love but I haven't finished yet," she said. "This is all I have so far. It's called Love: Love is important, for you and for me, for every step of love... maybe it should be 'every step *is* love'...." Claire tilted her head thoughtfully. "I'm not done yet."

"Some songs take a long time to finish," I said. "Poems are like that too." Claire agreed. She put my notebook, with the copied poems, into my book bag.

"I made some illustrations, too," she said. "You can look at them later."

The next day, my sister and I watched Claire and Audrey recite the Two Promises: "I vow to develop understanding in order to live peacefully with people, animals, plants, and minerals. I vow to develop my compassion in order to protect the lives of people, animals, plants, and minerals." The girls were given the Dharma names Pure Polar Bear of the Heart and Luminous Polar Bear of the Heart. We were as teary-eyed as any parent or aunt at a school graduation. "I don't know how much they will remember," my sister said, "but surely this can only be good for them."

At the end of February, I received a short letter from

Claire thanking me for some money I'd sent her as a Valentine's gift. I called her to acknowledge her lovely letter. Her first words on the phone were, "Is Thay still healthy?" I assured her that he was.

"Good," she said, and then proceeded to tell me about the submarine she was drawing at that moment with her grandmother. "It's like a map," she explained. "You can see all the rooms where the sailors live and eat and sleep. They are exploring the deepest part of the ocean so they can protect it better." My sister had said she was very concerned about the environment.

"That's great," I said, imagining the detail with which Claire was constructing her submarine quarters. Then I thanked her for the letter she had sent me. It was on the counter in front of me and I smiled again as I read the carefully composed prose. Her spelling had, for the most part, greatly improved with second grade.

Dear Aunt Nancy,
Thank you for the five doller bill because I can donate it to the animal shelter. Thank you for thinking about me on Valentine's Day. I am doing fine in school. I am studying the snowy white owl.

Love, Claire

Like all of our children, Claire is a continuation, part of the Sangha that will help to heal our world.

we have
arrived
we are
home

11: We Have Arrived, We Are Home

Thich Nhat Hanh

Your Happiness Is Here

WHEN I WAS in Massachusetts, leading a retreat, I went to the hospital to have a check up. The doctor said that I had an infection of the lungs and should stay in the hospital for a two-week treatment. I realized that the infection was possibly from the time I had spent in Vietnam, where I'd worked very hard. The doctor recommended I begin the treatment immediately that very night. But the Massachusetts retreat was still going on and I had three more talks I'd planned to give and three more walking meditations to do. I consulted with the other monks and nuns who were with me, and we decided that we'd finish the retreat before checking in to the hospital. The retreat went very well.

After the retreat ended, I went back to the hospital and began treatment at midnight. I was given two very strong antibiotics and four intravenous injections every day. I was allowed to go out of the hospital one hour a day for walking meditation.

Because I was in the hospital, I missed the retreat that I'd planned in Colorado, One Buddha Is Not Enough. Almost one thousand people had come to the Colorado retreat expecting to see Thay. Some were disappointed, sad, and worried in the beginning. Some had to leave. From the hospital, I got regular updates about the retreat and I sent messages to the participants.

The monastics and the laypeople practiced very well in Colorado, and in the end, many people said that the retreat without Thay was the best retreat they'd ever had. Transformation and healing was available for everyone. The Sangha has grown up. There is no reason to worry about the future of our practice, for us and for our children. One retreatant said, "Thay, you have a good sense of humor. We need more Buddhas. You are there and we are here."

After fourteen days, the lung infection has stopped. For twenty-one days, I rested and didn't give any talks. This morning, I asked my lungs whether I could give a Dharma talk and my lungs said, "Well, let's try."

The whole time I was in the hospital, I had many moments of happiness. As Buddhist practitioners, we should be able to bring *in* a moment of happiness whenever we want. We should be able to bring in a moment of relief whenever we need it. Can you tell a moment of happiness from a moment that is not happy?

In Massachusetts, I had a very interesting dream. It was very simple. I'd woken up at 1:30 in the morning because of the jet lag; 1:30 would already be the beginning of the morning in France. I decided to go back to sleep, because the sky was still dark; you can't do much at that time. I went back to sleep and dreamed that I woke up and looked outside and saw the sky was blue. I was very happy about the blue sky and that it was morning already. There was a young monastic brother nearby, and I saw that he was very excited. I asked, "What is the excitement? Why are you so happy?" He said, "I'm happy because my brothers from far away have just come home, and the atmosphere in the practice center is so happy." I felt the spirit of connection that is at the foundation of this kind of happiness.

The young brother was preparing a meal so that everyone could eat together in the spirit of family. Because the sky was so clear and blue, I went for a walk. I noticed the vegetable garden was beautiful and there were pine trees all around. I was remembering and

experiencing again the happiness that I'd experienced as a young monk in similar surroundings.

After some time, I woke up. It was only 2:30 in the morning and the sky was still dark. But the dream continued to bring me a lot of happiness because I could see what was in the dream in the present moment. In the present moment, there is also brotherhood and sisterhood, and the loving relationship between student and teacher. We can recognize moments of happiness that are available every day and every hour.

We can recognize a moment of happiness when the moment is there. That is the practice of mindfulness. It's only with mindfulness that we can recognize our happiness. Very often happiness is available, but we don't recognize it. With the practice of mindful breathing, we are able to recognize the many moments of happiness that happen in our daily life. We are just washing vegetables or just boiling the water to make tea. But with mindfulness, we recognize that this is a happy moment, and then happiness comes just like that.

We should be able to tell a moment of happiness from other

moments. When we walk together, when we sit together, when we breathe together, we can recognize that these moments are moments of happiness. The practice of mindfulness, the practice of concentration and insight can provide us with moments of happiness whenever we want or wherever we are. A moment of happiness is always possible with mindfulness, concentration, and insight.

When my lung infection ended, breathing in and out became very pleasant. When the lungs aren't infected, we can deeply enjoy our in-breath and out-breath. I've really been enjoying breathing in and out in the last few days. Breathing in, we can enjoy the fresh air that's coming in, nourishing our body. Breathing out, we can smile. Because I've just gone through a difficult moment, I can see and feel the contrast very clearly. When our lungs are healthy and strong, we can deeply enjoy our in-breath and our out-breath. When our lungs are infected, we enjoy it less. But many of us with healthy lungs don't enjoy breathing in and breathing out. We take it for granted unless the health of our lungs has been taken away and then comes back.

So happiness has something to do with unhappiness. The memory of unhappiness can be useful. Every time we think of that unhappiness, our happiness stands out very clearly. Happiness and unhappiness inter-are. Without the mud, we can't grow lotus flowers. So whatever unhappiness we have gone through may be useful for us to use as a comparison so we can recognize a moment of happiness. Our happiness is recognized against the background of unhappiness.

Those of us who have gone through a war know the suffering caused by war. Every day, every night, people die. You are aware of that, and your heart is bleeding because of that. During the Vietnam War, on Christmas day in 1968, both warring parties in Vietnam had a ceasefire for seventy-two hours. When the ceasefire started, all of us who lived there felt relief. We felt that now human beings could breathe in and out more easily and the grass and the trees could breathe easier as well. We hoped that there would be more days like that, so that people could stop killing each other. The hours of the ceasefire were very precious to us. We had experienced deeply

the suffering of war, so we knew how to treasure the moments of peace.

The Vietnam War has ended, and people in Vietnam don't have to die every day and every night like they did during the 1960s. We should be able to enjoy that peace. Perhaps those of us who have lived through the war enjoy the peace more than the young people who were born later on.

When we have a fever, we can't go out and do walking meditation outside. We have to rest. We're too weak to enjoy walking. We hope that we'll recover soon and can go out and enjoy a walk. If we can remember the moments and hours when we suffered from our flu and fever, we'll be able to enjoy our well-being and the opportunity to walk and breathe outdoors.

The Buddha teaches that it's possible to be happy right here and now. In order to be happy right here and right now, we have to be able to recognize the conditions of happiness that are already available. Our lungs are healthy. If we remember that, we'll enjoy breathing in and out; we'll enjoy our healthy lungs. We have a healthy heart, a heart that functions normally. "Breathing in, I'm aware of my heart." This is a condition of happiness. Mindfulness helps us to touch the many conditions of happiness that are inside and around us. Every time we touch a condition of happiness like that, we have a moment of happiness. We have many physical and mental conditions of happiness.

Suppose in the morning we brush our teeth, and we choose to brush our teeth with mindfulness. We may practice brushing our teeth in such a way that happiness and freedom become possible during the time of tooth brushing. We don't do it just in order to finish it. We may focus our attention on our teeth. We can treat them as our children, very gently, as though we're massaging them with a lot of love and with the awareness that we have healthy teeth to brush. That will bring a lot of happiness.

There are states of well-being within our body. When something goes wrong in our body, when there is some pain in our body, we may be caught by that pain and forget that other parts of our body are still functioning very well. Mindfulness helps us remember that even if there is some pain in one part of the body, the other parts of the body are still healthy. It's very important to focus our attention on those other parts. Mindfulness can also recognize and embrace the pain and bring relief.

The same thing is true with our mind because our mind is like a garden. Even if there's a tree that's not very healthy or is about to die, there are many other trees that are still robust, healthy, and beautiful. We have to be aware that, as a whole, the garden is still beautiful, so there is well-being. If there is not enough well-being in the lungs, but there is still well-being in the kidneys, the liver, the heart, that's a very good thing to remember. The healthy parts of the body will come and support the part that is not so healthy.

Mindfulness can help us recognize this, so we don't sink into anger or despair just because something's not going well in our body or our mind. Mindfulness helps us to recognize what is still good, healthy, and sane in our body and in our mind. And mindfulness helps us embrace tenderly the part that is ailing so we can bring relief. It's very important to recognize the well-being of every part of our body. It's also very important to recognize the well-being of many mental formations in us. To be happy, we need to be mindful. When we're mindful, we touch the many conditions of happiness that are already there inside and all around us.

A Spiritual Family

Mindfulness helps us recognize our happiness. But how can we generate mindfulness? We cannot buy mindfulness in the marketplace. Mindfulness grows when we have a spiritual home and a spiritual family. A Sangha, a practice community, is a spiritual family. When a Sangha is a true Sangha, when a family is a true spiritual family, it means the Dharma is there. Without the Dharma, a Sangha cannot be called a true Sangha. A true Sangha is a community of people who know how to practice in order to generate the energy of mindfulness, concentration, insight, brotherhood, and sisterhood. They are capable of bringing in moments of happiness for the healing and transformation of the whole Sangha. Members of the Sangha know how to breathe, how to walk, how to sit in order to generate the energy of mindfulness, concentration, insight, and how to transform and heal. This means that the true Sangha carries within herself the true Dharma. So Dharma and Sangha inter-are. You cannot take the Dharma out of the Sangha. Because the Dharma is the soul of the Sangha.

What is the Dharma? There is the spoken Dharma. There is the written Dharma that we can find in books. But the best kind of Dharma is the living Dharma. It doesn't need to be spoken or written down. When you practice mindful breathing, mindful walking, mindful sitting, you bring peace and serenity into yourself, you get understanding and compassion, and you radiate peace while you walk, sit, and speak. Love, understanding, and peace can be seen, and that is the living Dharma. Every one of us can radiate the living Dharma by our practice.

Look at someone who is walking peacefully. Every step she makes is solid, free, and healing. Each step is a miracle. She is performing the miracle of the Dharma, because every step she makes like that heals herself and heals the world and brings peace, concentration, and insight. She doesn't say anything, she doesn't write anything down, but she is radiating the living Dharma. When we see a practitioner practicing like that, we know that she is a true member of the Sangha. Her way of building a Sangha is through her practice.

The best way to build a Sangha is to practice the Dharma. When we come together as a spiritual family, as a Sangha, the best thing we can offer the Sangha is our own practice. We know how to breathe, we know how to sit, we know how to smile, we know how to release the tension in our body, and how to handle the painful feelings and emotions. This is the living Dharma that we offer to ourselves and the Sangha. The living Dharma is the soul of the living Sangha. We cannot take the Dharma out of the Sangha.

When the Sangha is a true Sangha, the Buddha is also there, because the Buddha is a human being like us. If you want to look for the Buddha, the safest place to look is in a human being. The Buddha is not a god. The Buddha is a human being, who has suffered, who has practiced, and who has developed his understanding and compassion. He has proved that understanding and compassion are possible, that happiness is possible. The Buddha is someone who has practiced the true Dharma. Since every member of the Sangha is trying to practice the true Dharma, everyone in the Sangha is a Buddha—if we're not yet a full-time Buddha, we're a part-time Buddha. So the safest place to look for a Buddha is in the Sangha, because the Sangha is made of human beings.

In Colorado, people had to look for the Buddha in places they did not expect. They found the Buddha in themselves and in the Sangha around them. One lesson we can take away from Colorado is not to look for your happiness in one person or one set of conditions. Your happiness is there in the community around you, your happiness is there inside of you. It is available any time. It is available right now.

Acknowledgments

THIS ANTHOLOGY was made possible through the gifts of many Sangha members. With deep devotion to Thich Nhat Hanh's direction, Sister Dang Nghiem skillfully guided our project while collecting letters, stories, photographs, calligraphy, and Dharma talks from the lay and monastic communities. Michele McCormick helped organize and format all the materials and Peter Poulides worked hard on the photographs of the banners and get-well cards. Thank you to Ong Lam for transcribing the monastic Dharma talks and to Mr. Dat Nguyen for translating Thay's hospital diary.

We thank Sister Chan Khong and the monastics who stayed in Boston with Thay at the hospital to care for our teacher and who shared their photographs and stories of that amazing time. During a time of political upheaval, we are grateful to those who kept us updated on the unfolding situation of oppression in Vietnam with the Bat Nha monastics. Finally, we are most grateful to our respected teacher, Thich Nhat Hanh, for continuing to breathe through his recovery and for being our inspiration to become "Buddhas-to-be" as we breathe the living Dharma together.

Parallax Press, a nonprofit organization, publishes books on engaged Buddhism and the practice of mindfulness by Thich Nhat Hanh and other authors. All of Thich Nhat Hanh's work is available at our online store and in our free catalog. For a copy of the catalog, please contact:

Parallax Press
P.O. Box 7355
Berkeley, CA 94707
Tel: (510) 525-0101
www.parallax.org

Monastics and laypeople practice the art of mindful living in the tradition of Thich Nhat Hanh at retreat communities worldwide. To reach any of these communities, or for information about individuals and families joining for a practice period, please contact:

Plum Village
13 Martineau
33580 Dieulivol, France
www.plumvillage.org

Blue Cliff Monastery
3 Mindfulness Road
Pine Bush, NY 12566
www.bluecliffmonastery.org

Deer Park Monastery
2499 Melru Lane
Escondido, CA 92026
www.deerparkmonastery.org

The Mindfulness Bell, a journal of the art of mindful living in the tradition of Thich Nhat Hanh, is published three times a year by Plum Village. To subscribe or to see the worldwide directory of Sanghas, visit **www.mindfulnessbell.org**.